Extra CREDIT!

EXTRA CREDIT!

8 Ways to Turn Your Education Expertise into Passion Projects and Extra Income

LANESHA TABB

NAOMI O'BRIEN

JB JOSSEY-BASS™
A Wiley Brand

Published by John Wiley & Sons, Inc., Hoboken, New Jersey.
Published simultaneously in Canada.

For general information on our other products and services or for technical support, please contact our Customer Care Department within the United States at (800) 762-2974, outside the United States at (317) 572-3993 or fax (317) 572-4002.

Wiley also publishes its books in a variety of electronic formats. Some content that appears in print may not be available in electronic formats. For more information about Wiley products, visit our web site at www.wiley.com.

Library of Congress Cataloging-in-Publication Data

Names: Tabb, LaNesha, author. | O'Brien, Naomi, author.
Title: Extra credit! : 8 ways to turn your education expertise into passion
   projects and extra income / LaNesha Tabb, Naomi O'Brien.
Description: San Francisco : Jossey-Bass, [2023] | Includes index.
Identifiers: LCCN 2022031459 (print) | LCCN 2022031460 (ebook) | ISBN
   9781119911067 (paperback) | ISBN 9781119911081 (adobe pdf) | ISBN
   9781119911074 (epub)
Subjects: LCSH: Education—Vocational guidance. | Teaching—Vocational
   guidance. | Career development. | Internet in education.
Classification: LCC LB1775 .T23 2023 (print) | LCC LB1775 (ebook) | DDC
   371.1—dc23/eng/20220803
LC record available at https://lccn.loc.gov/2022031459
LC ebook record available at https://lccn.loc.gov/2022031460

Cover Design: Wiley

SKY10036055_091422

Contents

Chapter 4: Online Learning: Developing Courses, Memberships, and Teaching Sessions   71

Hosting online (or in-person) summits, hosting your own conferences and live trainings— on your own or with a group.

Chapter 5: Virtual Services   97

Using your talents (or habits— like social media scrolling) to do things like taking photos, social media marketing, organizing, and writing/ ghostwriting for others scaling their own business.

Chapter 6: Becoming an Author 111

Teachers read hundreds and hundreds of books— professional books and picture books. Share your knowledge or your idea in book format via one of multiple publishing avenues.

Chapter 7: Public Speaking 137

Take your "show" on the road! Using your expertise to speak to educators at conferences, summits, and professional development opportunities.

Chapter 8: Passion Projects   155

Turning your extracurricular passions into a business.

Chapter 9: Exit Ticket   173

Index   187

Introduction: What's Your Thing?

If you've picked up this book, then you're in some fashion an educator who is interested in bringing in some extra income for whatever reason (because that's your business) and you might be looking for some guidance on where to start. Well, over the past 10 years, we have found ourselves in a unique situation where not only have we found multiple ways to earn extra income while in and out of the classroom, but we also have grown a huge network of educators that we now call friends from all over the country (world, even) who have done the same thing in their own way! We've been amazed at some of the ways that educators have found fresh and innovative ways to share their expertise. . .and we hope to highlight some of those here. And here's what we love about writing this book: the primary focus (for us) isn't just about making money. . .but rather finding ways to use your gifts, knowledge, passions, and expertise to share with the world in a way that makes you feel fulfilled. . .and how *that* can also bring in extra money!

We are hoping that if you're the kind of educator we think you are, we can speak to you with the assumption that you have an idea or you are at least open to discovering your idea. This means that we won't continually include caveats for educators who aren't looking to share their ideas with others and make extra income.

But we have a lot to share before we dig in.

First, EDUCATORS SHOULD BE PAID MORE. Speaking as teachers who spent plenty of years struggling to confidently pay bills, save, and invest—we know that there are systemic issues at hand. We have joined and continue to join the fight to change legislation that affects funding and get the right people in power who can bring the change we need to see in public education. We know that the way many educators are compensated is outrageous considering how important it is to prepare students for their futures. We can go on about this but, honestly, one fact remains: these bills are due. Period. These bills are due, and if you've got kids, then you know that those kids have the nerve to want to participate in every (expensive) sport under the sun, and oh, yeah, student loans are a thing for many of us. It's an awful position for us to have to be in, we know. And multiple things can be true at the same time. We can be disappointed with how educators are paid and grateful for the option to be able to launch a business venture and bring in much-needed income. We suppose it depends on you and how you want to look at it.

While we are on the topic of money, we do want to take a minute to qualify some phrases that we'll use around the idea of money. We may say things like *extra cash* or *income*, and while they have very different connotations, we mean money on varied levels. To us, *extra cash* incites some ideas of having money for your coffee habit or Target spree, whereas *income* feels like a larger, more substantial amount of money that can supplement or even replace income. We mean it all. Whatever your goals are, that's what we mean with those terms!

Also, THIS BOOK IS JUST A STARTING POINT. This book will not be an exhaustive list of every way to make some extra cash or exactly how to do so. This book is going to be full of our own stories and some examples from other people we know.

We're guessing that we are going to have two types of people reading this book. First are those of you with your shiny, new, exciting venture that is probably already brewing in the back of your mind. Are we right about that? Surely you've dreamed at some point about starting your own business. Maybe you've peeled out of the parking lot after school and thought about how proud you felt of that one lesson that you slay every year and wished you could bottle it up and share it with others. There's bound to be something like that that you've been mentally flirting with for a while, right? Okay, so that! That is what this book is for. We want to help you grow that idea that's been swimming around in your head by showing you tons of options for ways you can share your passions with the world.

And for those who may be sitting here reading this and thinking, "What are they talking about? I don't have anything like that swimming around in my head. . .yet," well, we wrote this book for you too!

We will ask you a few questions, and you can jot them down in a notebook or literally right here in the book. Pretend that we are out for a coffee date and we are asking you about yourself.

- What is your "thing"?
- What are your coworkers constantly coming to your classroom for?
- What is something that you see (a book, a lesson, a strategy) and you think to yourself, "I could totally do that better"?

So, let's take the first question: "What is your thing? Personal, professional, random. Doesn't matter. What's your thing?"

Why does this matter? Because a lot of times, your "thing" is connected to a passion. Passions, if you would like them to, can be turned into ventures that can bring in income. What if we told you that the teacher who loved pets created an entire resource

EXAMPLES

A teacher at my old school was next-level obsessed with pets. She had pets all over her classroom. Everyone knew that this teacher loved pets.

A school counselor at an old school of ours was known for his style. Came dressed to the nines daily. If "look good, feel good" was a person, that would be him.

A principal whom we knew absolutely loved to go all out for everything. Holidays, teacher appreciation week, you name it. . .it was themed, no details left unattended, and fabulous.

for educators who were interested in having a class pet? A guide with tips and concerns to think through when deciding on which pet to have, schedules for caring for the pets, and more. This educator had the knowledge and the passion. . .all they did was find a way to package it up and share it!

Similarly, consider the school counselor with style who snaps an amazing photo of his daily looks. But these aren't just selfies—that person is actually teaching others how to style looks for their body type—which might make them feel more confident. There are brands that love to work with people who have a natural knack for style, and they are willing to pay.

Finally, the principal who loves a theme. What if we told you that that passion for making people feel special became a blog that began with her sharing a few photos here and there—but turned into a platform where hundreds of people went to download fun, thematic printables that they could use in their own buildings?

Those are just a *few* examples of the kinds of ventures that are possible—and we can't wait to dig into more.

1. What are your coworkers constantly coming to your classroom for?
2. What is something that you see (a book, a lesson, a strategy) and you think to yourself, "I could totally do that better"?

OUR JOURNEYS

So, this is where we'd like to share an overview of our journeys. In this book, we dig deeper into a few of these ideas that we mention, but the point is that we've been able to gain financial freedom through some creative ventures.

LaNesha's Journey

I began this journey in 2011. Like so many educators, I had figured out that there were teachers who had begun sharing their classroom happenings on a blog. I had a handful of bloggers whom I followed religiously! I would teach all day, come home, and hope that Babbling Abby (aka Abby Mullins—a good friend of ours and the first teacher I ever followed) had posted something new from her classroom. Seemingly overnight, but probably more like over the next two years, teacher blogs exploded. Seriously—they were popping up everywhere. Eventually, we started to see amazing lessons being showcased, but then toward the end of the post, you would see a little button that said "Click here to purchase!" Now, understand: the things that I would see that were available for purchase were not things that I *needed*. No. I was given everything I needed in order to do my job. If I hadn't purchased a single thing from another educator, I would have been just fine. This was a personal purchase for something that I *wanted*. I make that distinction because I'm aware of the fact that many people believe that the concept of other educators selling lessons or resources is wrong and that we should all share things for free. I hear that, but for me personally, I didn't mind because the resources that I wanted weren't critical to the success of my students. I'm talking about an adorable "first day of school" activity or a fresh take on how to teach a spelling pattern. Did I absolutely have to have those things? Nope. Did I choose to buy them because I thought I would enjoy it? Yep! That's the difference for me. I firmly believe that educators shouldn't have to spend a single cent of their own money to do their job. But, listen—if you are the kind of educator that would rather swap your latte money for a print-able bulletin board set created by another teacher. . .then that is YOUR business! I digress. Back to the blogger boom—the point is, all of a sudden we had thousands of teachers who were setting out to share their ideas on the internet. . .and you could also turn that into a business if you wanted to. And, I did want to! I somehow went from barely being able to format things in my word processing program to somehow learning how to alter code in my blogging website to create an adorable template for my own blog. I began sharing my daily happenings with photo-graphs (which was a big deal back then as we were still using digital cameras and uploading the images, ha!).

So, I'm blogging away and then eventually, I created my first unit in 2011. It was my take on how to teach fractured fairy-tales (which are picture books that have a spin on the original fairytale). I created printable activities and wrote out a step-by-step plan for how to implement it. I made it available online for others to purchase for $5 and I couldn't believe it when I made my first sale! It was invigorating.

As time went on, I started to see other teachers get real serious *real* fast. I began to feel like the market was quickly drowning in lots of the same kinds of resources. Let's take apples, for example. I loved teaching a unit around apples to my first-grade students. We would read apple books and do apple-themed worksheets; I would put math facts on apple cut-outs and have the students record them on apple-themed paper (oh, to be a young teacher again). A part of me thought, "Well, I'm creating these things for my own classroom anyway—I should just post it and maybe bring in a little extra money to help with our bills." It was at this point that I made my first mistake. I didn't create it or post it to be purchased. Instead, I looked online and saw about a million other apple units—and they looked much better than anything I had made. I got discouraged and basically gave up. I thought, "Who needs another apple unit?" If I could go back, I would shake 2011 LaNesha and scream, "Post the apple unit, woman!" Because what I would come to learn over the next few years is that there *is* room for *my* version of something. I learned that there will be certain educators, daycare owners, stay-at-home parents and caregivers, and homeschool families that really appreciated *my* spin on a resource. Instead, I took a few years off—barely creating anything because I thought I wouldn't ever be able to be as good as these other amazing teachers. So, while I feel like I missed out on some critical years to create my version of resources that I felt were oversaturated, I do believe things happen for a reason—and eventually I found my stride.

A few years later, and as I grew in my experience, I began to notice the kinds of things that teachers in my buildings began to come to me for after school. They'd ask how I ended up with such great scores on my spelling tests or how my students were so well behaved during my lessons. I found myself coaching up my coworkers (who had asked) and began to take note of the topics that they'd ask about. That's when I had the thought that if these amazing teachers were looking for support or new ideas, maybe others were too! Even if I couldn't keep up with what I thought of as these incredible online blogger teachers—I could still help *someone*. And so I jumped back in. I started to compile how I was teaching spelling, reading, writing, and more. I gathered my original activities (because it's definitely not cool to repackage something that already exists and claim it as yours) and started to share free and paid versions on my blog. I would create a blog post that would give someone all of the nuts and bolts for doing the activity on their own—but if they didn't want to do all of that, they could also choose to purchase it from me. It went on like this for a while. I began to build out my library of resources and ended up with hundreds of units or activities that I shared.

Now, here is what you have to understand. This took time. *A lot of time.* This is why you'll see pushback in the battle that I mentioned before about whether or not educators should sell resources. If educators are sacrificing hours, sacred time away from loved ones, children, and so on to create something that will bring joy to another educator or save them time. . .then, yes, they will want to be compensated for that. And also, we all have the right to *not* purchase things. For one thing, there *are* tons and tons of free resources available for educators to download and use. But if one educator chooses to spend time making creative resources available to buy, then not only is that right, but also there is no rule requiring anyone to purchase it!

This is now the point in my journey where I truly began to operate in my purpose and passion. I found my niche—the thing that I felt that I could truly do better than anyone else (in my opinion). It came to me during the 2016 election season while I was teaching kindergarten. After a series of troublesome events unfolded (without getting into it, think: political sound-bites being hurled around by students, parents, communities) and a very specific and problematic conversation in my kindergarten classroom, I realized that something was missing from my curriculum: social studies. That journey is fleshed out in our book *Unpack Your Impact*, but that was the starting point for my niche. It was at that point that I reached out to Naomi and asked if she would help me create some social studies lessons that would celebrate culture, tell untold historical accounts, and include global perspectives through topics like economics, civics, geography, and sociology. She said yes! From there, we began to think about the lessons that we wish we had when we were little. We started researching firsthand historical accounts and debunking things that are taught without question in the primary classroom (like the "first Thanksgiving"). I taught the lessons to my kindergarten students in Indianapolis, and she taught the same lessons to her first-grade students in Denver, and we would rush home almost daily to share stories and conversations that our 5- and 6-year-olds were having. We would casually share these happenings on our social media platforms and over time, the interest grew. "You're doing THAT with kindergarteners? Your first graders understood that?" Those were the kinds of questions we started to get in our comments and direct message in-boxes. Say what you want about social media (because we certainly have lots to say about it—both good and bad), but we found social media to be maybe 70% joy and 30% a necessary evil. Sharing on social media took us from being a couple of teachers sharing their journey to the (admittedly self-proclaimed) go-to teachers for real, authentic, primary social studies. We wanted to be the teachers that other educators thought of first when they wanted to shake up their social studies content. The more we shared, the more we found our "people." We found the haters too, but they aren't hard to find. Don't focus on them. Focus on the impact that you can have on educators! We get more into social media later in this book, but social media brought eyes to our work.

We were being asked to share at conferences, professional development days, and podcasts. The moment that changed everything for me was when a teacher came up to me after I presented on our social studies journey in 2019. She said that she'd been planning to resign teaching not long after this conference we were at because she'd lost her passion for it. She was only there because her school had paid for her to go. She told me that because I shared my story, she was completely reinvigorated to get back in the classroom and make some serious changes. Y'all! That was all it took for me to know that if I can impact someone in that way, so can you. We can't take the power of inspiration for granted. Your story, your passion, your excitement for what you do can inspire others and literally change the course of someone else's life.

I'd narrowed my niche down to writing and social studies because those are the two areas that I feel the most passionate about—and those are the two areas that I've received the most feedback from other educators on how much it has helped them. I found that the more I created, the more I shared, the more opportunities would show up. That kind of energy is infectious. What I loved was that we didn't set out to get eyes on our work when we first started. Inauthenticity isn't cute. . .and people can totally sniff that out. We literally just wanted to share because we were so passionate about it. We shared with the same fervor that came with 35 "Likes" as we did with 1,300 "Likes." And that's because the foundation was and is a passion. The income is a very fortunate byproduct, but it came much easier when it was attached to something we truly cared about.

We learned that you never know whose eyes might land on your work. You never know who is in the room in which you are speaking. What we do know is that if it is truly something you care about and love to share, the people who vibe with you will find their way and they will support your journey. And that is where you find me today as I currently sit to write this book. I've been given the opportunity to speak to thousands of educators all over the country, write multiple books, design my own "merch," hold my own virtual conferences, work with companies (huge and small), and honestly when I list it out like that, I can't believe it. Before I decided to share my passions, I can assure you that I was the teacher who went to work, was terrified to ever speak in front of my staff, and had no desire to be a leader of any kind. Someone recently asked me if I ever thought that I would be doing what I'm doing and without missing a beat, I said "Absolutely not." But I also say with certainty that I'm so, so glad that I am able to operate in my gifts. I spent such a long time convincing myself that there were no more niches, no more "corners" in the market to be had—but there were. I found something *five years* after I'd first started selling my resources that changed the game for me. Don't let your attitude make you miss your mission. More on having the right attitude soon but for now, remember: there is room for you and it's not too late.

Naomi's Journey

Travel with me back in time, because I want to set a scene for you. Imagine that the year is 2010. Common Core is about to be rolled out, Comic Sans is the Holy Grail of fonts, and "Teachergram" doesn't even exist yet. I was really beginning to find my stride in the classroom and quickly realized that all of the lessons I wanted to do didn't exist. . .yet. I found myself constantly hopping onto my computer after work to create something new or tweak something from my school curriculum to meet my students' needs. . .and while the need to do this was annoying, doing it was really fun! I loved adding my students' names to worksheets and main idea passages. I enjoyed creating centers that incorporated their interests and backgrounds. It was a creative outlet for me and it positively impacted my students and teammates. Creating resources to meet my class-room needs became a hobby of sorts that I did as needed throughout the school year.

Imagine my surprise when a fellow coworker mentioned that there was a website I could upload my resources on and make some extra money. I didn't think it'd be worth the effort or be very lucrative so I paid it no mind—didn't even bother to check out the website or anything. I remember thinking, "How much money could teachers really be making selling resources online—$5 or $10? I'm good."

The Naomi of today is looking back at 2010 Naomi, shaking her head in disappointment and heaving deep sighs of regret. I wish I knew what I know now and had started my journey to turn my passions into profits right away. I hope that this story is beginning to motivate you *not* to put off your dreams of doing the same for another day.

Okay, we are time traveling again (imagine a dreamy wave sequence).

Now it's a year later and I still haven't attempted to create a single resource to sell online, but it was still happening in my classroom and for my teacher friends as needed. Luckily, that same coworker from the previous year didn't give up on me, and mentioned again how great it could be if I tried selling all of the things they always saw me creating on this popular site they'd heard about. They even shared about one teacher in particular who was making more on the site than her teaching salary plus ours combined! I finally gave it a try, and over a decade later, I am so glad I did. What started out as a side hobby to help put gas in the car quickly turned into an amount that covered monthly car payments, which then snowballed into an amount that allowed me to buy a new car a year and a half later.

I was highly motivated by the idea of what could happen if I worked hard enough to achieve it. I would come home from work, teacher-tired to the max, and then still stay up past midnight designing printables, looking for clipart, downloading fonts, and brainstorming new ideas. While it was nice to make enough money to grab a new teacher cardigan from Kohl's or go out to dinner with my friends and splurge on dessert, I began to wonder if the time I was putting in was really worth it. I'll be honest with you—hearing that one teacher made a million dollars isn't what convinced me to continue devoting large amounts of time to creating resources. I'd already convinced myself that that was a once-in-a-lifetime kinda thing, and that something like that couldn't happen for me (and to be clear, it hasn't), but as I began looking into what other educators had earned on this site, I found my inspiration. My *why*. And she probably doesn't even know it. There was a teacher named Amy Lemons who had been shouted out in a newsletter around the time that I was debating on throwing in the towel or not. I told myself that I got in too late—that I was too late to establish my brand or my presence to make the kind of money others were making. I told myself they'd been doing it for years and that it would take me too long to "catch up." But seriously, catch up to whom? I have grown to believe that the only person we should be in competition with is ourselves. I want to do better than me from last week, last month, and last year.

But I digress...back to Amy. I read about her in a newsletter and she was being celebrated because she had just reached a $75,000 milestone in her first year on the site! What struck me more than that amount in that short amount of time was that it had just happened a few months before I joined the site. That was the sign that I needed to keep going. This confirmed for me that success like this was possible for more than just one teacher, and it wasn't only for people who were well established on the site for years.

As the years went on, I continued to create resources that I needed because it turned out that other teachers needed them, too. A few years into my journey, LaNesha approached me with an incredible idea. She wanted to know if I would help her create a line of social studies resources. It was a brilliant idea, and I said yes, and the rest is history.

Our "thing" became social studies. Other educators began to come to us for social studies lessons. We saw what was out there and said, "We can totally do that better."

Somewhere along the way we realized that we could no longer run this business like a hobby. We began to get more intentional about our branding, or focuses, growing our social media presences and honing our crafts.

As I continued on in the classroom, I became certified to teach gifted and talented students. I began to incorporate this into my work and it was received well.

After year 6 in the classroom, it became abundantly clear that teaching students how to read was kinda my thing, so I decided to share more on social media about it and create resources to help others. It was also received well and I've presented on the topic for various schools and at conferences.

When I began to focus on issues of race and representation in the classroom, my resources reflected this new shift for me. I say all of that to say: your business can grow and change with you. You are your brand and your brand is you. Don't let others dictate what you decide to focus on and when you'll get started.

So, now you know our journeys that will give you a frame of reference for many of the other things that we cover in this book. Before we move on, a few more words from two people who have been trudging our way through our entrepreneurship (as in. . .it took us *years* to even call our businesses "businesses") on what you might want to keep in mind. With any business venture, it's a risk. You never know. But, here's one thing we've found to be incredibly important: attitude. We told you we'd touch on this more, so let's get into it. If you think no one is going to ever want to listen to you, buy from you, support you. . .then, they probably won't. We apologize if that seems harsh, but think about it—why would someone get behind your mission if you haven't even convinced yourself? It's so important to believe in what you are putting out into the world—but that is why it's critical that this comes from an authentic place. If you are just looking to "make some money real quick," this isn't the way. This is the reason we have been and will keep using the word *passion* when we talk about these ideas. We want to encourage you to draw on the gifts that you *already have,* that will aid you in the daunting fight against imposter syndrome. If you don't know what that is, definitely look it up—but long story short? It's the voice that gets in your head and says, "Who do you think you are? Who would ever want to listen to you? You're no one." But, listen. We are here to tell you that people are out here making money because they've decided to simply share what they are already good at— *with no one's permission.* Now, should some people be out here peddling whatever they feel like? Maybe not, but this is where responsible consumership comes in, too.

Consumers have the freedom to weigh the credibility, content, and quality for what they are buying. There is already tons of foolery out there for sale. Our point, or rather, our question is. . .whom exactly would you need permission from to do what you want to do? Share your expertise? Monetize your skill set? That was obviously one of the only ways to get it done in the past, but this day and age? We have options. So many of us spend so much time assuming that "we could never," but when you really start to research the beginnings of so many successful companies, you'll find story after story of people who just decided to make their own rules and do what they wanted to do. Like we mentioned before, our attitudes weren't *always* positive. We fight imposter syndrome daily. We spent YEARS not creating resources or not moving on a project because "everyone already created everything, so why bother" and still regret that decision to this day!

READY TO JUMP IN?

We hope you are ready to dig into the rest of the book! We want to set the stage for how the rest of the chapters are organized. We start the chapters with an introduction to the topic and discuss what it is and why it matters. We include some solid examples from us or our peers/friends who are using their passions to build businesses while inside and outside the classroom. From there, we dive into some pros/cons—some things to get excited about and some things to look out for because we want to keep it real with the difficulties that may come along. Finally, we share (where appropriate) some actual testimonials from us or other people who have been successful in their business who can offer some extra insight to their process for how they went about getting started. We cover the following:

Creating resources

Using what you are probably already doing to create resources that can help other educators.

Speaking

Take your "show" on the road! Use your expertise to speak to educators at conferences, summits, and professional development opportunities.

Designing "merch"

Merch is short for merchandise. How can you use your creative skills to design things like T-shirts, mugs, notebooks, and so on—without ever touching it?

Writing books

Teachers read hundreds and hundreds of books—professional books and picture books. You are capable to sharing your knowledge or your idea in book format and there are multiple options for getting it published.

Courses, memberships, online learning

Hosting online (or in-person) summits, and hosting your own conferences and live trainings—this can be done alone or with a group of educators that you pull together.

Tutoring services

You could teach summer school. . .or you could create a live or prerecorded service for parents/caregivers to sign up their children.

Virtual assistant work

Using your talents (or habits like social media scrolling) to do things such as taking photos, social media marketing, organizing, copywriting/ghostwriting for other people who are trying to scale their own business.

Personal passions

Taking your passions that aren't really related to teaching and making them work for you and your business.

The role of social media/email marketing

Taking "scary" terms like *marketing* and *branding* and making it super-simple. You can do it.

One thing we don't cover in this book, but feel to be critical, is the business-y stuff. We just want to put it on your radar. You'll eventually want to look into things like how to file taxes, LLCs/S-Corps, and other issues that will change due to you adding to your income. That stuff might sound intimidating if you've never heard of it. . .at least it did to us when we first began. This was a slow process for us because, well, personally, we are educators, not business people! We learned over time that having a working knowledge of these kinds of terms is helpful in having a successful and sustainable business. And that's what it is: a business. We are going to show you how these passions can bring you extra money, and when you earn extra money on your own, you're in business!

Are you ready? We are! Let's get into it!

Chapter 1

The Role of Social Media: The New Networking

Social media. The good. The bad. The ugly. Let's get into it.

If you were to hop onto social media right now, can you think of the one educator whom you always turn to for something specific? Maybe it's fashion, book recommendations, hot takes, or coaching tips. Whatever it is (and you possibly haven't even realized this), but for you, they have become the "authority" in that area. What does that mean? It means that with no one's permission, a person has positioned themselves in an online space to be the "go-to" person, the know-it-all, the *authority* on a particular topic. What topic do you teach right now? Middle school math? Can you, right now, bring a social media page to mind as soon as you think about middle school math? What made you think of that person? Could it be that they are *always* posting helpful content, images, book recommendations, strategies about middle school math? Or let's take it back to fashion. If you are thinking, "You know what? I'm gonna step it up in the outfits department," whom would you look to for fashion ideas? Whoever comes to mind has likely been making themselves the authority on whatever their niche is, and if you thought of that person. . .then it worked.

When you think about how you show up online, what have you crafted your space to be? When people come to your Facebook, Instagram, TikTok, or Twitter, what can they expect from you? Is it all educational? Some personal, too?

What can people expect from your presence on social media? (List everything you bring to the table.)

We want to share what we've noticed. The more focused you are, the better. Have you heard this old saying, "A jack of all trades is a master of none, but oftentimes better than a master of one"? That doesn't apply here.

You might be a jack of all trades; we get it. So are we. After a combined 25 years in the classroom, we definitely have more skills than what we highlight on our Instagram accounts, but when we started to take our businesses more seriously, we realized that finding a niche was important.

The goal is for you to be the first person someone thinks of when they open social media to search for ideas or content that they want to browse. Your community can grow so much quicker when people know exactly what to come to you for. If you want to be the authority on all things math, but half of your posts are your coffee order or you out with your friends, it may be hard for the audience you want to curate to see you as the go-to math expert. If you want an audience to learn from and possibly buy resources from you, they needs to know you, trust you, and see that you know your stuff. Conferences and brands are also browsing social media profiles to see who people are, and if they'll be a good fit for partnerships, solely based on what you consistently post.

What 3 (or fewer) things can you focus on to establish yourself as an authority and grow an audience?

1.

2.

3.

We know that many people have a love-hate relationship with social media. Trust us, we are with you. For us, some days on social media, specifically Instagram, can be an entertaining and wonderful place to share ideas and strengthen relationships with friends and educators around the world, and other days it's a complete dumpster fire.

Well, hate it or love it, we can't deny that it is also unequivocally the No. 1 reason our business endeavors have grown to be as successful and varied as they are. So, as follows, we lay out the main ways social media has been instrumental in our journeys.

SOCIAL MEDIA AND SUCCESS

When we first began selling our educational resources online over 10 years ago, we were very happy with the extra money we were bringing in, but it most definitely wasn't enough to support our families if we ever wanted or needed to leave the classroom. It was supplemental income, but our teaching salaries were what we and our families depended and relied on.

Once we started to begin to use social media as a way to showcase our resources, teaching talents, and passions, we noticed a number of things:

1. Our social media followings grew exponentially. We became the go-to pages for people who knew what to expect from us.
2. We began to connect with and form genuine friendships with like-minded educators (including each other).
3. We started to be sought after to speak at conferences and for school trainings.

4. Companies like Staples, Juicy Juice, Lysol, Ticonderoga, and HarperCollins began to reach out to us for partnerships and pay for sponsored posts.

5. We became privy to business ventures and ideas that we didn't even know existed.

Growing a Following

Like many other educators, we created teacher Instagram accounts to keep our teaching lives separate from our personal lives. We started our accounts and began sharing random quotes, our favorite teacher outfits, cute work from our students, our coffee orders, and our newest bulletin boards. Through Instagram's "Liking" format, it quickly became clear to us what people liked seeing from us, and what they didn't care for.

It took some time to find the "thing" that would really resonate with people, but before long, we did.

You can generally count on us to keep it real, so in the spirit of keeping it real, we want to share something we noticed years ago on Instagram: even though we were posting similar content to other educators on Instagram, we didn't seem to get the same amount of likes, engagement, or reposts as they received. We saw what was working for others, so we gave it a try. We had the cutesy posts, we had the bright classrooms, and we even made a pattern with our posts to make our feeds more aesthetically pleasing. You know, where you have a picture, then a quote, then a picture then a quote? Yeah, that didn't really work for us. When you aren't a part of the dominant culture, you'll find that, unfortunately, you may have to work a little harder to stand out. It can feel frustrating and disheartening to know you're sharing good content, but realize something superficial is what's holding you back from excelling. What finally worked for us was when we began to show what we were good at and we showed it consistently. Naomi was good at talking about representation and racism and how it showed up in the school system. LaNesha was good at the writing process and getting little kids to do big things. And we were both good at making accurate social studies lessons more accessible for young learners. Once we became some of the only primary educators in our little corner of the internet who were posting about things the way we chose to post about them, it was hard to ignore. We both became go-tos on Instagram for these topics because we were sharing what we were passionate about and we shared how other educators could tap into those passions as well. Engagement was up. People reposted us constantly. We had finally arrived! So whether it was a post, or a story, or a resource, or a blog, we began to find our people. We found people who began to trust us as educators because we had shown them over the course of months and years that we were the experts in these areas. Sure, the things that we choose to share are not all there is to us, but it's the way we chose to show up online. This choice led to many opportunities and allowed us to network and grow our businesses in ways we could have never foreseen.

Learning from Others

Social media has also allowed for us to see other educators in action and learn from them. We have been able to use social media as a professional development (PD) starting point. When we have seen educators share innovative ideas or practices that we hadn't been introduced to yet, we followed and learned from them. We listened to what they had to say and then did our own research. We found ways, when applicable, to add their expertise to our own teaching practices and classrooms. In addition to the professional gains social media has allowed us to have, we have also been able to use it to learn about the variety of ways we could grow our own businesses. When we first started turning our creative ideas into resources we could sell, that's literally all we did. We took our unique lessons and ideas, packaged them up, and sold them as downloadable files on the internet. It wasn't until years later, through social media scrolls and connections, that we realized educators were doing more than uploading and selling Portable Document Format (PDF) files. They had multiple streams of income and they were all connected to education. We were constantly left saying, "I had no idea people were doing that!" We talk about these multiple streams later on in this book, but to name a few now, we learned educators were making courses, building email lists, offering memberships, ghost-writing blogs, designing resources, editing, becoming virtual assistants, selling merch, and either joining the businesses of other educators or hiring teams for their own business. It was next level and it was honestly inspiring. Once we saw all of the possibilities. We wanted in! Maybe not immediately because it can be a bit much to try to take on a ton of new things all at once. But it was definitely something that helped us realize there was a whole world of more that we could tap into when we were ready.

Making Connections and Networking

Say what you want about social media, but we can't deny its power to bring people together. As millennials, we grew up being taught not to talk to strangers on the internet, but here we are writing a book telling people to use the internet to make connections with strangers on the internet. We wouldn't even know each other if it weren't for social media.

We firmly believe that if you put your personality and expertise out there, your people will find you. We have been able to use social media to find friends and professional partnerships all through Facebook and Instagram. We have found that DMs (direct messages) and comments here and there can grow into genuine friendships over time.

The friendships we have been able to start and maintain with people who live across the country have been incredible, and the same can be said about the professional collaborations that have come from social media connections as well. We'll speak about this more in our individual journeys later, but we really need you to buy into what we are saying. All of the ideas and journeys we share throughout this book would not be possible without the reach social media can offer us all.

After we began to establish ourselves as the authority in the areas we wanted to be known for, we began to post consistently. We began to think of ourselves as our own brand. Even though we had business names (Education with an Apron and Read Like a Rockstar), we didn't think of ourselves as a business or a brand for years, and we often separated ourselves from our brands and our posts reflected that. When we started to think of LaNesha Tabb and Naomi O'Brien as brands as well, we were forced to be more intentional about what we were posting and how we showed up on our Instagram accounts. We got pickier about what was going to go in our feeds because we were becoming more business minded. . .or we were trying to anyway. We'd like to think it helped because soon enough, schools were finding out about what we had to offer from their educators who followed us online and were asking us to come to work with their staff for PD trainings. Principals were booking us for consulting sessions. Publishers reached out to us to promote their books, but also to write books for them. Finding our niches and putting ourselves out there genuinely also allowed for conference owners to see what we could bring to the table and more speaking opportunities opened up for us.

Expanding a Hobby into a Full-Blown Business

While it was never the driving force or goal of our work when we first got started, we both ended up taking our businesses to a level where what was once supplemental income became an annual salary that matched, and then quickly surpassed, our teaching salaries. It was something to be proud of and simultaneously frustrated by because we know that as educators, we deserved so much more. Once this shift happened and our "hobby" was bringing in more than our chosen profession, we had some serious and tough decisions to make.

Now we like to joke that we are CEOs of our business and we get to do what we want, but let's be clear about what it takes to turn educational passions into profits, especially when you are first starting out. Yes, you get to be the CEO, but you are also the accountant, the secretary, the editor, the social media manager, the graphic designer, the assistant, the consultant, the marketing team, the graphic designer, the content creator, the researcher, the photographer, the videographer, the product tester, the head blog writer, and everything else in the company! It is a lot! So, when we had to make a decision about returning to the classroom *and* running our businesses or stepping away from the classroom to run our businesses full time, we had to schedule a very important meeting. When we met with our accounting team (which was us and our husbands), it made sense to hang up our beloved and well-worn classroom teacher hats, to give our businesses what they hadn't had in almost 10 years. . .our undivided time and attention. We were in the classroom the entire time we grew our businesses to what they are today and it was hard. We had to juggle many responsibilities at work and at home. We can't even count the number of nights spent uploading resources, creating Instagram and Pinterest posts, and editing social studies ebooks, and then still showing up for kids the next day bright-eyed and bushy-tailed with our lessons and data on point.

Now that's not to say we have stepped away from the classroom forever. We loved being classroom teachers and we still do. Currently, from time to time, we brainstorm about how to make both jobs work again in the near future. Teaching is a passion that will stay with us forever, but how we teach, where we teach, and whom we are teaching may change from year to year to year, and we are okay with that.

OUR JOURNEYS IN SOCIAL MEDIA

As you'll come to find out in-depth later on in this book, we create resources, we have published many books, we have courses, we've hosted our own virtual conference, we present at other people's conferences, we sell merch, we run a social studies club, we collaborate with brand-name companies, we have our own websites, we've run virtual summer camps, and so much more. We'll tell you right now, without a doubt, none of that would have happened without the power of social media. So even though there have been days when we wanted to delete our accounts forever and never look back, we have got to give props to a key player in our success: Social Media.

Naomi's Journey

My go-to social media spot for my business is most definitely Instagram. I've recently started to branch out to TikTok and I've dabbled on Facebook in the past, but Instagram has my heart. I began on Instagram because, well, that's what I saw everyone else doing. I had already been creating resources online for a few years, but the selling game evolved, like it always does every few months. All of a sudden, teachers were leveling up and marketing through Facebook ads and on their Instagram feeds. One thing to know about me is that I am a creature of habit and I hate change. So even though I saw other people starting to market heavily on Instagram, I didn't do it for the longest time. I wasn't at a place where I was really considering myself as a business, so I didn't think it was for me just yet. As someone who deals with anxiety, taking on too much at one time can quickly overwhelm me. I didn't step into using social media as a marketing tool until I was ready. Like we mentioned earlier, it didn't work out for us at first. But after I stepped into the role of being a go-to person for talking to young kids about race and racism as well as social studies content, I began to notice steady growth. People were coming to learn from me and with me, and I was proud of that. I was really enjoying the space I created and met some amazing people along the way, including partnerships with conferences and publishing companies.

Enter the summer of 2020. As if dealing with a global pandemic wasn't horrific enough, we were witness to a lot of harm caused to the Black community, and many people decided to collectively step up in a way they hadn't ever before. How did this impact me? Well, my Instagram account that I had organically grown for six years to about 30,000, gained about 100,000 followers in a matter of weeks. Let that sink in. Put yourself in my shoes. Now, a lot of people might be excited about that growth, but for me, it didn't feel good. I didn't know where all of these people came from. I didn't know if they were educators or not. I didn't know what they expected me to post. . .but they sure started to let me know. I began receiving hundreds of

DMs a day, and it was more than overwhelming to keep up with. Instagram was no longer a fun place for me to share my lessons and ideas; it was now a place where an audience of 137,000 strangers were demanding that I teach them everything about race, calling me slurs in my DMs, yelling at me in my comments, and expecting me to post about every situation happening in the world or they would post about me in their stories for not caring enough. Meanwhile, I had just had a baby, was dealing with my husband working with COVID-19 patients during the height of the pandemic, mourning with my community over the loss of Ahmaud Arbery, Breonna Taylor, and George Floyd, and homeschooling my kindergartener. It was hard for me to continue to post what I wanted and use my account as a business tool for my brand because my new followers had a lot of opinions and made it their mission to make sure I knew them. In the midst of all of this growth, bigger brands began reaching out for paid partnerships. It became a weird space to navigate. I wanted to share things that I actually cared about, but I also didn't want to pass up business opportunities. It wasn't good for my mental health, and I decided to step away. I reached out to a woman I knew who was doing anti-racist work that was similar to what I believed people came to my account for. If they were there for that content, I wanted them to get it, but it just couldn't be from me anymore. So, after warning this woman about what she was getting into, I handed it off and started over. I made a brand-new account called ReadLikeaRockstarTeaching, and redefined what my content was going to be. I share all of this to remind you that you should be very clear about what your account will be and what you want to share. Set boundaries with your followers and stick to them. Also, keep your block hand strong. You do not have to engage with everyone on the internet. You do not have to deal with harassment. You do not owe everyone every aspect of your life. Yes, you should use your social media to show what you know, but don't let it consume you. It can quickly become a lot, but your mental health is more important.

I am happy with my new account because I am able to post what I love and show up in a way that feels healthy for me and can positively impact my business. I feel that I have helpful ideas and content to share in a way that really resonates with people and helps children. I love being able to help caregivers and educators navigate concepts. I get DMs from people saying their school has used my blog posts, resources, and Instagram posts to help plan PDs at school. I've also worked closely with caregivers to give them tools they need at home to help their children become stronger readers. Moments like that really make my day and remind me that Instagram isn't the worst after all.

LaNesha's Journey

It was Instagram for me. Twitter, I quickly realized, has a much more serious vibe where lots of educators thrive and that's great! You may find that that is where you might fit best. That was not the case for me. I wanted to share in a way that felt more free and fun, so Instagram was the place that felt closest to my blog when I got started. I feel as though I'm too old for TikTok (but who knows, maybe I'll try it out one day) and Facebook has always been frustrating for me, so, yeah. . .like I said: it's the 'Gram for me. I used to be @anotherdayinfirstgrade, but that was stifling because I wouldn't always be teaching first grade. Eventually, I changed my name to Education with an Apron or @apron_education because I loved to wear cute, frilly aprons (with pockets) while teaching at school! I thought it was catchy and memorable. I became widely associated with aprons and that's what I was going for—easy recognition.

The Instagram thing happened quickly. All of a sudden (after years and years of blogs being the go-to place to follow educators), teachers began to transition their personal Instagram accounts to "teacher" Instagram accounts. It was so lighthearted at first. Cute activities or bulletin boards were all the rage. It was so much easier to post your classroom happenings on Instagram because you could post a photo and a caption, which is way faster than a full-blown blog post! I joined in the fun. I'd share books that we were reading or a cute selfie in my apron. Slowly, Instagram grew to be a place where we could build relationships with educators all over the country. It was so easy to find other educators whom you could relate to. If you were looking for inspiration or even professional development in a post, this was the place. I started sharing resources and ideas, but it was all over the map. I'd share a reading activity one day, and a meme that I'd screenshotted another day, and maybe my new living room furniture arrangement the next. It was a hodgepodge of whatever I felt like sharing. I started to notice that other teachers were using their account for marketing purposes. I noticed that people started to include a logo or a watermark on their pictures. They started to use branded colors and fonts. I slowly began to make that shift in my own social media presence.

Eventually, I decided to really focus on my passion, which was/is social studies instruction. We dig into the details of how I found my niche in a later chapter, but I had one goal: become the authority on that topic. How did I become the "authority"? I (along with Naomi) started to share book quotes, activities, and free resources all around the idea of bringing real, authentic topics into the primary classroom. I collected stories from my classroom and experiences that were extremely powerful that would happen when we would encourage educators to try these strategies and topics out with their students. It just became our "thing." I would post about other things occasionally, but I tried not to let a holiday, heritage month, or any seasonal topics go by without posting our "spin" on it.

My audience grew over time. Mostly, I attracted people who could resonate with what I was posting—and that's really what you want. You want to find your people. You wouldn't want to curate an audience that has no similar interests because it won't be very likely to engage with you. If you're trying to share your passions with others, then that should be the driving force behind your social media. While we felt like we were growing well on our own, the summer of 2020 drove my (and many of my friends' accounts) to numbers that we didn't ever see coming—and honestly, didn't ask for. Without all of the details, lots of people shared our accounts and told people to go follow us, which was honestly not as fun as one might have thought it would be. We went from natural and steady growth to, well. . .a lot. All of a sudden we were "teachers with a platform" and "teacher influencers," which made us really confused because we were the same teachers that we were before our accounts suddenly grew. We were literally minding our business and then suddenly it felt like we were no longer allowed to make mistakes without being "called out" or expected to learn about everything (global events, specific causes) and post about it in real time.

Why am I telling you this? For one thing, it's a cautionary tale. Just as you are likely sitting there thinking, "I don't think that would ever happen to me," we thought the same thing. The other reason is because we can use this opportunity to explain what we've had to tell people who send us messages to speak on something that is important to them: we all have voices. We do. We've told people to post about their cause on *their* pages and they'll typically respond with "Well, I don't have the platform that you do!" *How do you think platforms are grown?* You post. You raise awareness. More people join in. As we write this book, I have seen this play out before my eyes with the Science of Reading. There are some teachers who may have had a smaller following who began to post consistently about how most of us are incorrectly teaching students how to read. They make videos, share quotes, all the things—and their accounts are blowing up. They decided to raise awareness around the topic that is important to them and people gravitate toward it. That's literally just how it works. We all have a voice and you can't count yourself out because people who go viral often say that they never thought it would happen. It happens all the time.

For me, social media is almost like that friend whom you enjoy and they've had your back—but if you let them, they will suck all your energy and have you throwing your back out while you try to attempt the latest dance trend. Except you're not trying the latest dance trend on a wild night on vacation with your crazy friend. . .you're doing it online. You've got to be careful with those friends, right? Because if you're not, you can easily get wrapped up in doing all kinds of social media related things (that aren't even always necessary), so you've got to be careful. Just like when you're with your wild friend—have fun but also have a level of awareness that will keep you grounded. I've had to make rules for myself around what I'll respond to and what I'll stay away from. I've even put time limits on how often I'll let myself on. You have to put some parameters in place because if not, social media can really affect your mental health.

With the same breath, I'm forever grateful for social media. I have best friends (whom I speak with daily) all over the country. I've been able to network in ways that I couldn't even have imagined just a few short years ago. I've also been supported by my online community through devastating losses, and life's highs. I've been sent thoughts, prayers, care packages from people whom I've never met before and who will likely never know how much those things have meant to me. I've been able to do the same for people I've followed and have grown to care about like family. Say what you want about social media, but for me, it's not all bad. A lot of it is really, really good.

THE PROS AND CONS OF SOCIAL MEDIA
The Pros

We've said it so many times, but we really love the connections we've been able to make. We wouldn't know each other or a lot of the people who have become our good friends without it. We have been able to use our platforms to share ideas and practices we were successful with in the classroom to help other educators and parents positively impact children. Networking is so much easier because of social media. We are able to make connections and learn from people with the scroll of a finger. As entrepreneurs, it's a great marketing tool that allows people to see the information we know and the content we create. Once you have a community that is in alignment with your purpose, then showcasing your resources becomes easier because there are people who love what you do. It's a relatively quick and visual way to talk about our brands. And honestly? A lot of times, it's just plain fun. People are funny and creative. It's so easy to be inspired if you've curated your social media to give you a positive experience. We feel as though you really do feel a sense of community after a while. We've watched teachers get married, start families, and send those same babies off to second grade— all while having never met them. We've seen how, through social media, people rallied around and supported educators who have survived tragedies, battled illnesses, and lost loved ones. Social media has lots of qualities that make it worth it if you create that experience for yourself.

The Cons

We both touched on this in our individual journeys but the pressure and the labels from other people can grow to be a bit much. You'll have to decide how to deal with DMs and rude comments. Don't get us wrong, the positives definitely outweigh the negatives, but when an internet troll says something that catches you off-guard, it can really throw off your mood for the rest of the day. As much as we'd like to sit here and say we don't care, we do. We are human. Someone we don't know being extremely rude, or in some cases racist, to us out of the blue does affect us for a period of time.

It's an interesting space to navigate. You want to grow, gain followers, and connect with more people, but the more you grow and gain, the more you open yourself up to possibly being attacked by people you will never meet. And that's the thing to keep in mind. It is important to take in some criticism and honestly ask yourself if it's valid. You might find that you have posted something wrong or problematic and you do need change it or do better. But if you've reflected and checked in with yourself, and it turns out it's just a miserable person looking for some company, block them and keep it moving. Some people and situations are just not worth your energy. You've got a business to run, so stay focused!

TIPS FOR GETTING STARTED

As you continue on through this book, we hope that you will keep the role of social media at the forefront of your mind. No, it doesn't have to be a part of your journey at all if you really don't want to for your own valid reasons, but we have personally found it to be the best way to put ourselves out there.

Social media has helped us find an audience to connect with, collaborate with other educators for friendship and business purposes, partner with big brands for paid partnerships, and find out about other business ventures we would have otherwise never known about.

- Find a niche and stick to it.
- Establish yourself as the go-to person for your niche.
- Post often.
- Make sure your posts are visually appealing.
- Be your authentic self so that people can connect with you.
- Engage with your followers and others doing similar content.

Chapter 2

Designing and Selling "Merch"

We don't know about you, but we believe that all educators are creative in some way. You have to be if you're working with kids. Don't tell us that you don't get creative in some way with classroom decor, relationship building, making schedules, lesson planning, and new initiatives at school. You know you do! It comes with the territory. It's the reason people love to tell us "*Whew, I could never be a teacher!*" We've got that magic. Don't count yourself out because you aren't creative in the traditional sense of the word. You probably just need to learn how to activate and rethink your creativity to produce different kinds of projects.

In addition to being creative, we know that all educators have their own personalities, sense of style, and sense of humor. With over 85 million teachers worldwide, there's bound to be some teachers who share your sense of style or humor, so why not try creating merch (short for *merchandise*) for them? Most educators love merch. We love a good teacher T-shirt, jean jacket, and pencil pouch. Do you enjoy a bright and cheery aesthetic? Or simple and minimal (seriously, look at the Rae Dunn empire)? That can all translate into your style for designing merch, and it's going to resonate with some.

Have a brand/business? Great! You can add merch to the list of things you sell. Don't have a brand/business? Great! You can add merch to the list of things you're going to start selling. You may be one idea away from creating and selling merch, and it may be easier than you ever thought it could be! From mugs to totes to aprons, to T-shirts, we've sold it all and we want to share how with you (see Figures 2.1a and 2.1b).

Figure 2.1a The black apron and navy-blue T-shirt pictured were created by us and are sold on our websites.

Figure 2.1b T-shirt designs by Naomi.

So, when we say *merch*, we mean anything that you create or design and sell that isn't a digital or physical educational resource. Over the years, we have added merchandise to the list of things we sell because, honestly, the name of the game for us is having multiple streams of passive income. Just having one side hobby may meet your financial goals for extra income, but if you're anything like us, over time, you'll begin to branch out and see what else you can get going that makes money for you (sometimes with minimal effort on your part) and is helpful to others.

When we have talked with friends and colleagues about getting into selling merch, many of them are apprehensive. The No. 1 reason people give us to explain what's holding them back is the judgment they may get from other people.

Listen. Other people do not pay your bills. Other people could turn out to be your biggest supporters. Other people should not dictate the way you live your life. We don't mean to sound insensitive. We get it. We really do. But we really want to remind you that it's your life and you have permission to do what you want. Pursue your passions and do what makes you happy. Make that mug. Design that candle. Start that T-shirt line. Market those earrings.

Merch Ideas (What's your thing? What do people come to you for? What have you seen that you can improve? What's a need you have/had?) Don't worry about the logistics just yet. Dream Big!

1.

2.

3.

Now, let's design it! Draw out some ideas. . .now! You didn't plan on becoming a fashion designer, did you? That's okay—you are about to be one now (and earn another stream of income). Let's go! See Figures 2.2–2.4.

Figure 2.2 Design your t-shirt ideas here.

Figure 2.3 Starting dreaming up a catchy mug phrase that educators will love.

Figure 2.4 Design a tote bag that every educator needs.

We don't want to tell you to dream big and then leave you out in the cold. In this book, we aren't just talking the talk, we have walked this walk. Everything we are speaking about is something we are currently doing or have done in the past.

OUR JOURNEYS DESIGNING AND SELLING MERCH

What we do now is share about our journeys and let you know about all of the merch we sell and how we've marketed it.

Naomi's Merch Journey

I feel like we say this a lot throughout this book, but please believe me when I say that when I first began my career in education, I never thought part of my job would be designing and selling other educators merch that they actually wanted to buy. As my social media was growing and my resources were reaching more educators, I really tried to begin thinking of myself as a brand and more of a business. I wanted to branch out into other ways to make more money for myself and my family. (Now don't let that deter you from starting your own merch line just because you feel like you don't have the right amount of followers or online presence. There's no magic number. You can start right now.)

Whenever I would post a hard-hitting quote on social media, I always got a couple of comments like, "Can you put this on a shirt?" or "I would totally wear this if it were on a shirt." For a while I paid the comments no mind. I just took them as a compliment and that was the end of that. Even if I wanted to turn my quotes into shirts, I didn't even know how to make it happen. In my mind, I would have to ship a ton of shirts to my house, purchase some machine to press my designs onto the shirts, and then print labels and get my stuff mailed. If you're anything like me, even just reading all of that exhausted you. But let me tell you what, when I discovered that websites like www.Printful.com exist, my merch prayers had been answered (see Figures 2.5–2.8).

Figure 2.5 These t-shirt saying were inspired by daily teaching life.
Source: Missy LuLu's

Figure 2.6
Source: ORION DESIGNS

Figure 2.7
Source: MariusTees

Figure 2.8

A term that I would like to introduce to you (if you aren't already familiar) that will change the game: *dropshipping*. I didn't know it was a thing. It's a thing. Dropshipping websites offer creators and designers a very easy solution for getting out their merch without doing a lot of work on their part. I have sold tote bags, shirts, and mugs using printful.com. I even designed a towel for my son's birthday, and all the merch has been great quality and sold very well. The way that Printful works is that I have to upload a picture or Portable Network Graphic (PNG) of the image that I want to use on the site. In order to do this, I go to my dear friend, PowerPoint, and play around with fonts and styles and quotes that I think would look good on a shirt or a mug or a tote. Keep in mind when you're doing this that people have to use these things. So maybe there's something that's funny in your head, but wouldn't necessarily sell on a shirt. You have to start thinking like a designer and thinking like a seller. Put yourself in the consumers' shoes. What would you want to buy? What would you feel comfortable wearing out and about at work or in another place? Sometimes people create items that are funny to look at, but other people don't necessarily want to buy. A funny or powerful slogan has the potential to sell well, but you have to make sure that it's well placed and looks good when you put it on the T-shirt. Googling a font-pairing guide can help you in this aspect and assist you with your aesthetic if you're having trouble determining what looks good.

For a few of my designs, the shirt that I made would also double well as a mug or a tote so I can use the same PNG and use the same phrase or design on multiple objects. With sites like printful, the sky's the limit: you can create canvases, hats, flipflops, and even fanny packs (Figures 2.9 and 2.10).

Figure 2.9
Source: Dark Haus

Figure 2.10
Source: DESIGN DISCO

Maybe you are the type of person who is more hands-on. You should definitely go that route and make it happen. It may cost you a bit more money up front because you have to buy the products and supplies that you need to get started. You have to take care of the shipping costs and you are responsible for getting everything out on time. If that fits your work style and personality, then I say "Go for it." Many people do it every day. Work to your strengths and follow your passions.

My best friend Lydia Diaz of Clever Girl Craftings creates and sells earrings and glitter-dipped Flair pens (Figures 2.11 and 2.12). She loves to work with her hands, enjoys packing up the products she designs and hand paints at home, and truly doesn't mind going to the post office a couple of times a week to mail everything. Using the power of social media is how she gets the word out about her earrings and pens, and she is able to work from home and earn extra income creating items that she loves.

Figure 2.11 Custom earrings created by a small business owner, Tiffany Diaz.

Figure 2.12 Personalized pens created by Tiffany Diaz.

With the use of my social media platform (Remember we told you how important an online presence is? It doesn't have to be huge, but it does help), I was able to quickly spread the word about my new merch. Using myself as the model, I took some pictures, uploaded them to my Instagram stories, and added a link to my website. If you don't have a website (like I didn't for years), there are other platforms you can upload your items to and sell from there like Etsy or Shopify.com.

Do you recall earlier when we said not to worry about what others think and do it anyway? I want to clarify that advice. I do it anyway, but I still worry about what other people think. I just don't let it stop me. The first time I was about to release the first shirt I designed, I did wonder what people would say. I almost let it hold me back from going for it.

I have many different crowds that follow me on social media, and the fear of judgment can be real. That impostor syndrome can sneak up and say, "Who do you think you are?" "Who's going to buy this design from you?" "Who told you this was cute?" And the answers to all these questions are: "I'm me. I never know who might buy it, so let me go ahead and try. And I think it's cute."

Sometimes I give in to letting the thought "But I'm *just* a teacher" hold me back. And that simply isn't true for me. I'm not just a teacher. I love being a teacher, and there is so much more that I have to offer in addition to being an incredible educator. I am a whole person. So if I want to be a teacher who creates resources, has a social media presence, and sells merchandise, then I'm going to be that teacher. Teachers are incredible. We can do it all if we want to.

I can't sit here and say that selling merch is my biggest source of income, but it is a source of income and that matters to me. I'm proud of my designs. I'm proud of my growing business. It makes me happy to be able to diversify my creative portfolio and continue to provide for my family in this way.

The cons of selling merch are pretty minimal for me. Sometimes I create something that I think will sell pretty well, but it flops. But honestly, the only thing I lost was 30 minutes of my time creating a design and uploading it to a site. The other con is keeping up with certain items being out of stock on the site. Printful is usually pretty good about immediately updating your inventory, but you may have a time when a customer orders something that is no longer in stock, and you'll have to put on your customer service hat to attend to their needs.

One more tip I have to share is to make sure you order your own items before you start selling them and make sure they look good. When I first got started, I sent myself one of my own shirts and the text was way too low on the shirt and it stretched too far on the sides. I had to learn where to place the text, and how big to make it, in order to get the best look in person.

LaNesha's Merch Journey

My merchandise journey is a little different. My friend Nicole (whom you meet a little more formally in our chapter about creating courses and memberships) exposed me to this idea of dropshipping. She had been selling T-shirts on her website, and I thought that was awesome but I had no clue how she did it. She went on to introduce me to a ton of websites that offer dropshipping options. They are amazing! You can literally log on, select a blank T-shirt, mug, tote bag, cell phone cover, literally tons and tons of items, and upload a customized image onto them. I decided to create T-shirts for teachers like me who weren't represented.

It all started when I was walking through TJ Maxx one day. I saw the most adorable T-shirts and tote bags that had a silhouette of the back of a woman's head whose hair was thrown up into a pile on top of her head. That image was accompanied by the phrase "Messy Bun, Getting Stuff Done" It was adorable, but the girl's image looked nothing like me. Her hair was nothing like mine. I decided that I was going to create something that I hadn't seen at that point. I started creating T-shirts with cute phrases that were applicable to my hairstyles. My very first T-shirt had the phrase "Lessons, Grades, & Box Braids." See Figure 2.13.

Figure 2.13 This saying was created because there wasn't anything like it for educators who wear brains.
Source: Equine & Design

I posted the tee on my social media channels and they took off! I was receiving emails and messages thanking me for providing an option for T-shirts where the images and phrases reflected these educators. From there, I became addicted. We (me, and surprisingly, my husband) came up with so many slogans that had to do with both school and hairstyles. I started to branch out and come up with tons of other ideas for teachers. Then I started hearing from the other professions that work in the school setting. The school counselors wanted to know where their T-shirts were. So did the administrators, speech pathologists, and school psychologists. I tried to create as many as I could because, like Naomi mentioned before. . .why the heck not? It was super-easy. Like Naomi said, we could design the images using the clip arts and the fonts that we refer to in Chapter 3 on creating resources, and we could save the image as a PNG. Chapter 3 reminds you that the background must be transparent. Once you save that image to your computer, you drag and drop that image onto the merchandise available on the dropshipping websites. It's literally the easiest thing. So, for me, that's where it all started.

Eventually, I started to dabble in having T-shirts printed and shipping them myself. I wanted to see if we could make more money if we took on some of the labor. While dropshipping companies are amazing, like Naomi mentioned, you don't always make a ton of money on them. It's definitely worth the trade-off because they are so easy to create, but I wanted to know if I ordered T-shirts in bulk and handled the labor, would I be able to keep much more of the income. See Figures 2.14 and 2.15.

Figure 2.14 T-shirt designs created for an underrepresented audience.

Figure 2.15 Aprons created
with simple sayings.
Source: Vect in

I had created a T-shirt that was a play on the television show
Black-ish. The year after the pandemic, we were all supposed to
be going back to school. . .but everything was so uncertain.
I decided to make a very simple design that said "Back to school-
ish" on a black T-shirt, and it took off (Figure 2.16). I posted it on
my social media channels, and the response let me know that
that was going to be a popular T-shirt. Instead of uploading it to
my dropshipping website, we contacted a local printer and asked
the company if it could cut us a deal if we ordered the shirts in
bulk. We quickly had to figure out how to print labels and navigate the U.S. Postal Service. While we did get to keep way more
of that income, we lost a ton of time, and honestly, patience
with each other. It was super-fun at first. We were like "Look at
us. . .over here printing labels and shipping out packages daily,"
but much like you read in Chapter 6 about becoming authors. . . .
Shipping out items can wear you all the way out. There's customer
service correspondence and shipping mishaps and other things
that will quickly allow you to see whether you are built for that
life. We aren't.

Figure 2.16

But, shipping might be for you! Maybe you do want to purchase a T-shirt press and create your own workshop. Go for it!
We have friends who press at home. They watched some
YouTube videos and invested in a machine that allowed them to
heat-press a design and took off (Figure 2.16). That's an option
for sure, but it is not what we chose to do. We love getting the
passive income on some designs that we uploaded and then let
someone else do the work.

We did have a phase where we decided to sell aprons and that
was because the year we returned after the pandemic, I was
looking for a way to have the masks, sanitizer, and antibacterial
wipes on me all the time. Our printers (that we'd ordered the
Back to school-*ish* tee from) told us that they had some black
utility aprons that could be customized. We stuck a few of the
designs we'd created on there and made those available. We took
it a step further and started to attach things like pom-poms and
ribbons to the aprons (Figure 2.17). This was fun but extremely
labor intensive. Not only that, but it was extremely difficult to
keep a steady supply of things like pom-pom garland on hand.

We would max out vendors at craft stores and it became very stressful. We still do some shipping from home, but not nearly as much as we used to.

Figure 2.17

SOME LOGISTICS

In this section, we get you pointed in the right direction so that you can begin your research. First, let's be sure that we have a big-picture understanding of how print-on-demand and drop-shipping models work.

Print-on-Demand

There are some websites that simply allow you to upload a design to a product (or multiple products) *for free*. Then, they allow you to post that product on *their* respective platform. A buyer could come across your design, purchase it, and you would get the specific profit margin that you would set up on the website. They'll ship it right to the customer. This is the easiest and lowest risk method to sell merch. Companies like this include Threadless, Zazzle, or Redbubble (research these websites to see them in action). This is easy, and you won't have to set up a website or anything to host your store. You would have to share out the link to that product to your community or someone might happen upon it and purchase it. The downside (if you want to call it a downside) is that your products are mixed in with a lot of other products. It may be hard to get eyes on your work. But, your product is for sale, and you can make some money with minimal work and zero investment! Some of those platforms allow you to choose your profit margins but many don't. That means that they will decide your profits at a fixed rate. This is something to look out for when deciding on a platform.

Dropshipping

Buckle up, dropshipping is similar but more involved. It's going to sound like a lot, but remember, this book is a launch-pad: a light introduction to a concept that you'll want to dig into and research! Okay, so dropshipping: for one thing, this is *your* store, so you'll get to decide your profit margin. You will need to host your store on your own website. This can be embedded on a lot of major platforms for websites (like WordPress, e.g.). It takes more work to set it up, but once it's done, it's done. It's also nice because your products will be the only thing people will see, so they won't be distracted like they might be on a print-on-demand site.

This option is also more expensive. That's because you'll need to purchase a domain and possibly purchase apps to help your store run smoothly and many of those run on a monthly subscription fee. Once you've got a domain (make sure it's memorable and easy to mention, so probably *not* something like "T3ACHERZROCK.COM"), you would then need to connect that domain to your store. Popular stores include Shopify or Woo Commerce. The ecommerce platforms will help you make that store look like, well, a store! You'll see that those platforms will include the codes that you'll need to embed on your website. So, essentially, you would need to begin researching domain options, dropshipping companies, and then how to connect those two. It's kind of a lot, we won't lie. But you've got the most rudimentary terms for where to start!

From here, we go at this from customers' points of view.

1. Customer makes a purchase from your store. They will pay retail price. If they buy a T-shirt from you, they'll pay you the $25 or so that you've charged.

2. From there, your store will automatically send their order to your supplier, which is your dropshipping company (because those are now connected). That company will get to work filling the order. It will print the T-shirt on demand, ship it, and you'll never touch it. The company also will take around $15 to cover the cost of all of that work. The rest of the money will be left for you.

3. Customers will receive their packages from your drop-shipping company, but the merch will be branded to look like it came from you (which it did, but only by way of them).

Like most of the chapters in this book, this is totally doable, but there is probably going to be a learning curve. However, in Chapter 5 about virtual services, we provide you with some other options. There are tons of "work for hire," open market-places that you can go to pay someone a one-time fee to set up all of this for you. You can post a job on a website like Upwork .com that says: "Need someone to set up my online store and connect it to my website," and someone will respond by telling you that they can do that in their sleep.

We like to try to figure things out on our own via the great World Wide Web, but if we keep hitting walls, then we might choose to outsource if our budgets allow for that. You'd also be surprised by who might be hiding in plain sight in your personal friends and family network. Try posting what you need on Facebook (if you're on Facebook) and watch that cool person you used to work with a few years back respond saying that they know how to do that very task. They may even take payment by way of a friendly dinner or coffee date. It's happened to us before!

THE PROS AND CONS OF DESIGNING AND SELLING MERCH

The Pros

It's fun! It really is. If you're creative, it's a great creative outlet. It's relatively low-cost and it can be very rewarding to see something you designed take off. You can meet a need by including a group that's often left out or make someone laugh with your ideas.

The Cons

You have to constantly market yourself. It can often feel inauthentic to constantly market your merch if are used to using social media for other purposes. Coming up with new and unique designs may be time-consuming. Ordering your merch to assess the quality of the shirt and how the designs look in person can add up and take a lot of time to get your merch posted and ready to sell.

TIPS FOR GETTING STARTED

- Sketch out some merch ideas in this book.

- From there, hop on to the design software of your choice (PowerPoint, Canva, etc.) and begin to recreate that design as an image. Grab an image of a T-shirt or mug, and so on (just for practicing purposes) from a stock photo website that you can design on. Then begin to craft the vision.

- Once you get your merch to a point where you love it, start making moves to get it on a website for sale. We've given you some key terms and websites to get started, and now it's on you to make it happen.

- Finally, remember: keep your attitude in check. From two entrepreneurs to you (the future entrepreneur): it's super-easy to get caught up thinking about how there are already 7 million T-shirts (pencils, stickers, totes, etc.) out there for educators. Well, guess what? Yours isn't out there yet. And your design might be what someone else is looking for.

We are waiting for you, 7,000,001!

Chapter 3
Creating and Selling Resources

If you've seen others creating resources and ever thought to yourself, "I could do that. . .if I knew where to start," then you're in the right chapter because we want to share everything we wish we knew when we first got started creating and selling resources. We hope that you use our tips, learn from our mistakes, and don't let that voice inside your head (or on the internet) tell you that you can't monetize your skills and talent just because you're an educator.

SHIFTING YOUR MINDSET

As educators, we give and give of our time and expertise until we exhaust ourselves. We even have a "cute" name for it: teacher-tired. If you've logged the hours (and it does take hours) and used your knowledge to create a resource and someone else chooses to buy it because they don't have the knowledge or the time or the skills to do it themselves, do not feel guilty about being compensated for it. I mean, we can have a talk about capitalism another day, but is that not how everything works? One person has a good or a service. Another has a need or a want. They should trade! It's been happening for thousands of years, and we don't have to be ashamed to join in just because we are in the business of helping kids. A desire to help kids doesn't pay our bills, but if a resource can, we're going to make it happen.

Who knows what educators need more than other educators? We've been there. We get it. Who among us hasn't had to give a side-eye to the "teach with fidelity" rule and modify a text-book company's curriculum to better suit their needs? We use our professional judgment day in and day out to provide our students with what we know is best for them. This is why creating resources for other educators to use can be such a beautiful thing. Thinking back to over a decade ago when we first started, our mindset was always, "If we need it, someone else might need it too." Like we said before, if you're just trying to throw together some random PDFs, charge a high price, and hoping to get-rich-quick, this isn't the line of work for you. But if you have some writing lesson ideas that you know guarantee student growth or you have an engagement strategy that you have perfected over the years or you've figured out an innovative way to assess the standards for your grade level, we say shoot your shot!

Another reason to begin creating resources is to create solutions to the educational problems you're seeing. For example, one major reason we love creating resources is to add diversity and representation to lessons. Back when we first got started, we weren't seeing lessons that included people that looked like us or our friends. We, as Black women, saw adorable resources popping up and the clip art and/or stock photos would almost always feature exclusively white people. If you have always seen yourself represented in everything (think movies, princesses images on backpacks and tees, commercials, lunchboxes, billboards, etc.), then you likely have never even realized that your identity was being affirmed since the day you were born. It's just normal to you. It's nothing for you to walk into a gym for a workout and look at the huge wall murals featuring white athletes working out and see that as normal. Just imagine walking into that same gym and looking up to find every model was Black or another person of color. You would immediately notice and wonder if you were in the right place. That's where the saying "representation matters" comes in and that is what we felt was missing in resources that students were being shown year after year! Hopefully you can see that for us, our problem was that we weren't seeing honest and accurate stories from history being told, and we wanted to provide diversity in primary content.

We noticed many students were going through their schooling with picture books, anchor charts, history lessons, and even clip art images featuring people who didn't look like them or their classmates. We've even noticed this in our own children's elementary music classes where the educator gave an overview of the composers that they'd be learning about and there was zero diversity or representation. There were only white men being learned about. So, think about it. . .if you're a music teacher who also wants to monetize their expertise, you could decide to create and sell units teaching about diverse styles of music and cover musicians who never get celebrated or acknowledged. Your resources could be picked up by schools, daycares, recreation centers, churches, or a musician who teaches lessons to children on the side!

Our point here is: keep your eyes open. What is the "thing" that bothers you and you'd like to take action to change? You can provide resources to people who are also looking to make those same changes! Look around; there are opportunities for improvement everywhere. Is there a lesson you teach annually that you always have to adjust because it isn't quite right? That could be your thing!

Now you might be sitting here thinking about an idea you have, but feeling like there's no way to turn it into a printable PDF (*PDF* stands for "Portable Document Format" and is just a way to reliably share a document with others). We want to stop you right there and challenge you to dig a little deeper. There's more to resource creation than just making worksheets. Could it be that your idea is better represented through a different medium? It's okay to be the blueprint. As a matter of fact, it's better to be the blueprint if you can manage it.

We want you to do us a favor and jot down three ideas that are swimming around in your head right now. Even if you can't think of a way to turn them into a resource at the moment, write them down anyway. Think about the questions that we ask you in the Introduction. Don't be afraid to dream big here. . .write it down!

Like we said before, worksheets are not the only types of resources that exist. All types of resources are needed by all types of educators all over the country and world. Yes, we know that many people create printable worksheets, tests, and crafts to put together, but you can be different. You can choose to design and sell ebooks, scripted curriculum, games, useful

> **Educational Ideas (What's your thing? What do people come to you for? What have you seen that you can improve? What's a need you have/had?)**
>
> 1.
>
> 2.
>
> 3.

videos, intervention materials, classroom decor, staff PDs, and more. (*PD* stands for "professional development"; it's used a lot in reference to things like meetings, trainings, or conferences.)

We have a friend who has her classroom management on point. She has amazing routines and procedures in place—even during the pandemic. This teacher knows how to train her students to be productive, helpful classroom citizens who truly care for one another. And it's not a fluke—she does this year after year. She is even asked to share about her amazing practices at school PDs and educational conferences. Once, when we were having a conversation about turning that passion into profit, classroom management was what she wanted to figure out how to "bottle and sell," but she couldn't think of a way other than just talking about it.

So, we started to brainstorm. What could she do? Then it hit us: she could make a classroom management for beginners training guide of sorts. She could include tips and coaching for other teachers. She could design a scope and sequence of her tried-and-true practices and explain how to roll them out with students. She could include a troubleshooting section to help educators solve commonly recurring problems that she had figured out how to navigate. She could also include posters, behavior contracts, incident reports, templates for corresponding with caregivers, and anything else a teacher might need to utilize. We thought a bit more and came up with what the students might benefit from. She realized she could create visuals for them. Chants to remember the procedures and routines, and a slideshow for the teacher to follow that the students could view and interact with. That's a resource! That's a product you can sell that someone would likely purchase! Good classroom management is a need many educators have. If you have a thing that isn't just a worksheet, don't let that deter you from thinking of ways to make it accessible for others.

We love to think of new and innovating ways to share our resources with educators so they can impact students. Creating ebooks (and by *ebooks*, we literally mean a PowerPoint presentation saved in a PDF file to be read as a book) was a game changer for us. We wanted to share accurate stories from history and create engaging activities to go along with them. The only problem was these stories did not exist. . .at least not at the kindergarten and first-grade levels.

We would come up with an activity that we knew teachers and students could use, but we also knew that there would need to be some front-loading before a student could access the content. We also knew teachers didn't have the time to just do the research themselves before using our activities, so we decided to do the work for them! We put in hours researching and fact checking to create digital books that educators could read to their students and get them the information needed to go along with the printables we designed.

Figure 3.1 Examples of product covers.

We know that when we were teaching lessons, we appreciated having quick access to all the teaching materials we needed, and we were willing to bet other educators would appreciate it too. So we compiled our findings, added headings, stock photos, and captions, and created our own ebooks. These books are one of the things that we are the most proud of when we consider all of the work we've put out over the past few years (Figure 3.1).

Figure 3.2 *Rosa Parks with Dr. Martin Luther King Jr.*
Source: United States Information Agency / Wikimedia Commons / Public domain. This is an example of a historical photo that is available in the public domain that can enhance a resource that you'd like to create.

Educators from all over the country have reached out to us and let us know how easy it has been for them to implement our resources and how we have become household names in the classrooms as the authors of the ebooks their students love to learn from. It means so much to have that impact.

Let's back up a beat. We are getting ahead of ourselves and jumping into the time in our creating lives when we were more established. We don't want to send the message that everything at the beginning was easy and perfect because it most certainly was not. We both deleted a fair share of resources that we created because we just had no idea what our style was back then or what was good enough to stock our virtual shelves with.

When we each finally decided to get our lives together and start uploading resources to sell, we quickly realized it was a lot more than just uploading the fun worksheets we'd been making for our students. If we were going to be putting our resources out into the world for anyone to download and pay good money for, they needed to be packaged well. They needed an eye-catching cover, directions for the educator who would be using them, readable fonts, appropriate and helpful content for students, and no copyright infringement violations. These requirements were a lot. It seemed daunting, but we went for it.

Remember, we've been at this for *years*. We've been able to experiment and slowly grow our expertise and craft over time. Hopefully that isn't discouraging but if it is, then remember: we all have to start somewhere! We have truly been able to reap the positive benefits of monetizing our expertise to help others and we've been thankful for the impact it's had on our lives.

OUR CREATIVE PROCESSES

Before we get you started creating, we want to walk you through our creative processes so you can see what you can glean from them. Before we jump in, here are few foundational things to note:

1. Fonts, images, clip art, borders, and so on must be purchased and labeled "for commercial use." You *cannot* just grab any image you see online and insert it into your document. *You will get sued.* Maybe. But I wouldn't risk it. There are tons of people who offer free and paid resources that are available for commercial use. We give you some phrases to use in your research at the end of this chapter.

2. Check out what is already out there. Google the very thing you are thinking about creating. If it exists, that doesn't mean you can't create it, but you will want to figure out what will set apart your resource. If someone is deciding which resource to buy, how can you make your version stand out?

3. Creating from your expertise will win you half the battle. We have been primary educators for basically all of our careers. We had people begging us to create resources for upper-grade students. We foolishly took that on for a month or two and ended up *hating* every second of it. Our ideas were solid, but we really struggled to think about what older students would do with it because that wasn't whom we were used to teaching. When you are creating from your expertise, you will know if it's age-appropriate or not. You will know how large or small the text or writing spaces need to be. And your audience can trust that it's coming from someone who can meet their needs well.

Okay, now that those things are out of the way, we want to share our processes with you. We co-create tons of resources, but we have very different styles of creating.

Naomi's Process

I'm an impulsive creator. I blame it on my ADHD, but it works for me. My process goes a little something like this: I spontaneously get an idea because of something I just heard, saw, or did. Then I instantly think about how I could possibly turn it into a resource. I think through the logistics, and whether it's needed and it's in my scope of expertise to be the one to make it. My brain starts swirling with creative possibilities. I think about the end result that I would like for students to walk away producing or learning, and then I backtrack, thinking about what I can create to get them there. Sometimes I wish I was more of a planner, but I'm not. I'm a do-er. When an idea like this strikes, it's imperative I get to a computer and start creating right away before I lose the idea or the motivation to design it. I start with a blank page and I always add a heading and a border/frame. That sets the tone for me (Figures 3.3–3.5).

Figure 3.3 Example of worksheet designs.

Figure 3.4 Example of worksheet designs.

Figure 3.5 Example of worksheet designs.

A good frame and heading makes that blank sheet a little less overwhelming to work with for me. I think about whether adding some clip art or an icon is needed to enhance the look of the design.

I then begin to think through the independence level of the age group using my resource and where I intend for it to be used in the classroom. Will it be best at a center, during whole-group, or at a small-group table? Sure, consumers can use it how they see fit, but my intentions help me have a focus.

I stick to a personal rule of using no more than three different fonts within the same resource so it can look cohesive and not too busy or distracting. I also consider the readability of the fonts for the students and educators accessing it. I think about the resources educators may or may not have, and I try to include everything they'll need. All of my teaching experiences were in underfunded schools, so I try not to assume that people will just have access to the materials that are flowing like water at other schools. It may be something you want to consider as well, or at least make sure you are up front about it in your product descriptions and product previews so people know what to expect.

I am usually creating for the K–3 grade levels, so I have to consider the audience. How big should my fonts be? What kind of writing lines should I include? How large should boxes for illustrations be? When I'm finished designing, I print my work out and fill it out myself or I have my son test it out for me. I want to make sure it looks good and serves a purpose other than being visually appealing.

The cover is the last feature I design. I get inspiration for the cover after I am able to see the resource in its entirety and capture what needs the resource will meet. I love to save my pages as a PNG (Portable Graphics Format) and insert the little pictures onto my cover. PNGs are crisp with great resolution so they really help my audience see what they're getting. I also use the PNGs on my description pages within the resource that I include to let educators know how my resource is intended to be used. I try to be as clear as possible so that they can download it and know exactly what to do with it.

Then I add in my copyright page (I just insert the same one each time), and it's ready to upload and share with others. I have one copyright I always use when I work with LaNesha and one for resources I create on my own. We'll talk more about these later, but feel free to use the same wording we did. Let anyone purchasing your resources know that purchasing your resource gives the user one license and that it shouldn't be copied or placed on the internet for free in accordance with the Digital Millennium Copyright Act. (See Figures 3.6 and 3.7.)

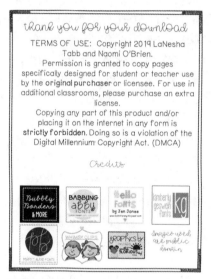

Figure 3.6 Examples of worksheet credit pages.

Figure 3.7

LaNesha's Process

Unlike Naomi, my process isn't very "step-by-step," although, at times, I wish it were. I'm more of a "grab an idea and sit in front of my laptop and see what happens" kind of creator. I have to find the right vibe/feel before I get started. I love to seek inspiration from creatives *outside* of education. A lot of times the resources that you will see for sale online can have a very similar look to hundreds of other resources. That's largely because there are font creators and clip artists who are extremely popular in this community, so it's hard not to have a similar look to another resource. I will often take my idea and sketch it out on paper first. I have to have a plan before I start working.

When I created my writing process units, the product was born when I got home from school and I'd been thinking about how awful my writing block was that day. I really need to teach my students how to be more independent. I kept thinking of a wall display that I could use to allow my students to move themselves to various levels of the writing process. On the back of my daughter's homework, I sketched out some arrows and boxes with notes and scribbles all over it. As soon as I have something like that, I can head to the computer and make it happen.

From there, my process is similar to Naomi's. I stick to the "no more than three READABLE fonts" rule, for sure. We used to have a blast with all of the various fonts because they were so darn cute, but it can make your resource look thrown together, and often it can make it very hard for students and children to read. It's always a good idea to create something that you've personally used with students or children. Sometimes I'll actually pay my own children to "work" for me by completing a new activity that we've created. It gives me a chance to work out the kinks and make sure everything flows as it should.

I always try to think through teacher directions. If an adult is going to use your resource, you want the process to be crystal clear. You can't just assume that the person using the resource automatically knows everything. For example, if I create a reading resource that asks students to focus on vocabulary, I'm not going to just tell the teacher to "have the students 'close read' the passage" because not all teachers even know what it means to do a "close reading." You don't have to be responsible for teaching everyone everything, but you can be more selective with your wording or you can even send them to a helpful blog post, article, or book to learn more about a concept.

Once my resource has been created and tested, I'll print a fresh copy, fill it out myself, and using my phone snap some photos of it. These can be used to showcase the product in a way that will allow a potential buyer to see exactly what it should look like and how it works. Then, it's ready to be posted (Figure 3.8).

Figure 3.8 Example of a product cover.

CREATING RESOURCES 101: PLANNING YOUR PROCESS

Though we have different processes with our creations, we both use PowerPoint to create them. You don't have to use PowerPoint, but it's relatively easy to learn once you figure out what you're doing, so we recommend you give it a try. (Wiley has published several books offering a step-by-step guide to PowerPoint.)

You may see the worksheets and books that we jump in with some broader, more logistical ideas for how to start creating resources. Remember, the goal is to take your expertise and use it to create a resource that will be accessible to most educators and students. The following tips will help get you started!

Headings and Borders and Other Things: So we already spoke briefly about a heading and a border or a frame. We both agree it can start your resource off right if you're creating a worksheet, test, or some type of printable. Shapes can be inserted to be used as response or drawing spaces. Lines can be added to create spaces for students to write. Don't forget to create a space for students to write their names and possibly the date. If you're worried about creating something that's already done, consider presenting it in a unique format that you haven't seen before. You can decide if your printable, ebook, or lesson plan will be portrait or landscape. You can use borders and headings to design aesthetically pleasing PDFs. Now, we know that something being "cute" isn't the goal in education, but remember, you're joining a competitive market. What your resource looks like does matter. Seeing a preview of your layout versus someone else's may be the deciding factor for another educator to choose to purchase your resource over another one.

Stock Photos, Icons, Clip Art, and Fonts: Depending on what you're creating, your resource might benefit from adding a photo, icon, or clip art. If you search for free stock photos, fonts, or clip art, you will more than likely be able to find something free that meets your needs, but we've got to be honest—some of the free items out there aren't always what's best for your resource. We think of it as investing back into our resources when we purchase things like this. In our experiences, paying to include well-drawn clip art or eye-catching fonts has always paid off. Literally. Consumers appreciate a well-put-together resource. Many clip artists and font creators allow their work to be used for free if you don't plan on selling it. But if you plan on selling resources with fonts and clip art, make sure to pay attention to their rules. They will usually outline how their work can or cannot be used. Make sure to pay attention to their licensing rules and always credit them properly. More about that in the Copyright Page section that follows.

Readability and Usefulness of Content: We urge you to consider the readability of the fonts and layouts you choose for your resources. We've made the mistake of creating meaningful resources, but using a font that wasn't practical. If you're creating a student resource that contains cursive fonts that look good, but the kids can't read any of it, the resource isn't going to sell well. And if it does sell, the feedback you receive may be poor. Consider the size of fonts and work spaces for students as well. Think about what students using your resource will be able to do with it. How useful is the product you're making and what will students walk away with when they are finished with it? How is student thinking being captured? How are they able to show their learning?

Another aspect of resource creation you may want to consider is including an Answer Key. When applicable, many educators would appreciate an Answer Key included in their resource for quick access to check student work.

Copyright Page: Any time you create a resource, it is incredibly important to include the copyright page. Many times the fonts, clip art, and stock photos will have requirements for you to include if you're going to use them as a part of your commercial product. Basically, if you're going to make money with the help of others' work, they need their credit—even if you purchased it from them. And rightfully so! If a clip artist works really hard to create a set of clip art and you use it in your product, somebody else who sees that product might want to know where you got that clip art from. The first thing they would do would be to check your copyright page. Oftentimes there will be a logo or a link that the creator will ask you to include on your copyright page. These pages typically are at the end of a resource. If you're using stock photos from a website that is free, check the permissions. The photo sources will normally specify if they would like specific credit. Sometimes a source will tell you that credit is not really necessary. You can definitely find plenty of free resources to include when creating, but you will find that you also may need to purchase some things like fonts or borders in order to give it a really nice and polished look.

CREATING RESOURCES 201: PRICING AND MARKETING YOUR CREATIONS

You've created a project that you're proud of. . .now what? It's time to figure out how to price it and market your idea. Over the course of our time selling resources, we have discovered and come to accept that the perfect pricing formula just doesn't exist. The perfect marketing plan doesn't either.

When it comes to pricing items, we definitely recommend comparing your resource to similar resources and seeing what others have done. Whatever you do, don't undervalue your work. We've seen some people make the mistake of thinking if they price their resources really low, they'll get a lot of sales. Yeah, you might, but listen, you deserve to be fairly compensated for your work. Also, it may cause people to side-eye your work and wonder why it's priced so low. Think about it like this: let's pretend you're at the store deciding between three different new laptops to buy. They all look pretty similar, but one is very cheap, another one is around the price you'd expect, and the last one seems to be overpriced, and you aren't really sure what features justify this price increase. Which one would you buy? For us, we'd end up choosing the laptop that was the most reasonable. The cheaper one might be appealing at first, but it would cause us to wonder what was wrong with it.

We encourage you to look at the final product and really think about it's worth. If you crafted 50 passages and corresponding comprehension questions, in our opinion, that's worth more than 50 writing prompts added to the top of lined paper with mostly blank spaces.

If we bought a new font, clip art, or frame to add to a new resource, we don't add that into the price. We consider it an investment. Educators purchasing your resource don't see that it took 20 hours to create and $15 worth of clip art or fonts to design the resource they purchased. All they see is the final product, and that is what we feel the pricing should reflect.

If you talk to enough educators turned creators, we are sure each one will swear by a marketing strategy that you just have to use, but you'll come to find that what works for others may not work for you. So while we can't tell you the perfect path to take, we can tell you a few things to look into that have worked for us and others.

1. **Social Media:** A good resource will speak for itself! Post about it, share it, and get people talking about it. If it's great and others love it, they'll share it too. You can use

videos, photos, or a combination of both to share about your resource.

2. **Pinterest:** Using photos or PNGs, create pins that others will see and repin. Make sure your pins are visually appealing and showcase your product well. Take a look at what others are doing to see which pins are the most popular. But remember, don't copy. Use others for inspiration, but find a style that fits you!

3. **Email Marketing:** This might sound intimidating, especially when you're first starting out, so tuck this away for a time when you feel like you're ready for it. If you've built up a pretty decent audience on social media or another online platform, you may want to consider collecting emails. How many businesses do email marketing? All of them. If it's good enough for Apple, it's good enough for us. We weren't ready for email marketing for quite some time. But when we finally dipped our toes in, we honestly wished we'd started it earlier.

4. **Facebook/Instagram Ads:** In truth, they work for some people, but they are expensive with little or no return on your investment. If you are just starting out, we would recommend saving ads for a later time, once you feel that you're more established.

THE PROS AND CONS OF CREATING AND SELLING RESOURCES

The Pros

We've said it before and we'll probably say it again: education is our passion. We admit, when we first started teaching, we envisioned being in the classroom for 30+ years. We never thought we'd be out of the classroom and working as teacher authors full-time, but here we are. Where we started and where we are now was never in our cards, but as of this moment, we are happy with the way things have played out. We can make incomes that help us take care of ourselves and our families, and we are still able to positively impact educators and students all over the country in a way we never thought was possible. We know that when we are adding the final details to a resource that it is going to find its way into a classroom where 20+ students are going to learn something and have fun with it. We love hearing from educators about how much time using one of our resources saved them or how their love for teaching a certain subject was deepened or revived after using a resource of ours. We love the ability to share our innovative ideas via blog posts or free resources to show educators a different way to teach a skill. We honestly love putting in the hours to create a resource knowing it's going to make the day or week or month a little easier for an educator. We are the definition of "love what you do and do what you love." It takes a lot of hard work, but for us, it's been worth it.

The Cons

Having done this for a few years, we would say that some of the things we don't love would be having to figure out ways to continually market. We get into some marketing concepts later in this book but generally speaking, it's difficult to sell anything without some marketing. It can feel weird to market your products to other people, but how else will they know what you have? There are ways to handle marketing that feel natural to you. You really just have to take some time and experiment with different marketing strategies. You might find that you love social media and sharing images there gets you the traffic to the product that you are looking for. You might find that you want to create a blog and simply post photos and an explanation of your resource on that blog. Much like anything else, no one will know what you have if you don't find ways to put it in front of other people. The great thing is, once a few people find your resources and begin to use them, if they decide that they like it, then they will share with their friends. Word of mouth can go a long way in this business. There have been countless times where I've heard one educator tell another educator that they just have to go check out resources by a teacher whose work they have come to really love.

A lot of times we will find ourselves in an interesting situation where people will suggest or offer unsolicited advice in regards to our resources. They may say something like, "I really love this resource, but is there any way you can remove this clip art so there are more lines for kids to write? That request may seem harmless enough, but it's difficult for people to understand that when you create a resource, certain things have to be generalized in order to be used by the masses. Not only that, but the assumption is that these resources were meant to be custom-made. It's not the biggest deal in the world, but it is something to look out for. Earlier in our journeys, we would actually try to accommodate requests like this. That just left us feeling frustrated and depleted because, if given the choice, everybody would want a custom detail implemented, and that just isn't realistic to keep up with. Now, you might find that some feedback is helpful and actually improves the quality of your resource. But that is a choice for you to make.

Finally, we highly recommend finding yourself an editor. You can hire someone officially or maybe you have an aunt who has always had a knack for grammar and syntax. What you don't want to do is put out resources riddled with typos. We've learned this the hard way. Earlier on, when we could not afford an editor, we spent tons of time correcting typos that people would email us about. It is a huge deal! If educators are going to trust you in purchasing your resource, the last thing they want to do is print out everything, pass it out to their students, and then find a huge typo. We cannot even lie to you all. . .we have been there! As soon as we were able to hire someone to read our work, we made that a priority. But this didn't happen for about 8 years—after we had a reliable source of income from creating resources and could afford to make the investment back into our businesses. Again, if you can't hire an editor (or don't want to), consider sending your resource to friends to proofread for you or just make sure you do a really good job hunting for typos yourself. We've even paid a coworker money here and there to read through a few things for us. Or we've traded the resource for editing from other teacher friends. Educators are creative and flexible; we are confident you'll find a way that works for you.

DREAMING UP YOUR CREATIONS

Remember, this is more than just creating "some worksheets." You can create so many things beyond just a worksheet. Here is a list (not complete, of course) of things we've seen created:

- Full units plans
- Printable labels for organizing
- Vocabulary cards
- Assessments
- Bulletin board borders that can be printed, laminated, and displayed
- PowerPoint templates that can be used to display lessons
- Name tags

- Kits with reference charts that can be printed and glued/taped on a file folder
- Flashcards
- Clip art (frame clip art)
- Plays
- Task cards
- Study guides
- Online learning activities (with moveable pieces)
- Meet-the-teacher presentation kits
- Bookmarks

...and literally anything else you can think of! The possibilities are endless.

If you still don't know what you want to create, we'll ask again: What do you want to create? What's needed by your students or other educators? What's out there that can be done better?

We firmly believe that if you're out there just creating stuff you *think* will make you money quickly or you try to throw something together you saw someone else do, it may not work out well for you. You've got to find your thing, and more importantly, you've got to meet a need. This is the beauty of being in the classroom or having a pulse on the state of education. We knew what was needed because we needed it too! Naomi remembers needing phonemic awareness and main idea resources that were engaging and easy to implement for her kindergarten and first-grade students. LaNesha couldn't find any resources that taught the writing process in a way that gave autonomy to kindergartners and really helped with internalizing the steps to becoming a real writer. And we both couldn't find real social studies for primary students anywhere. We looked high and we looked low, then we decided to just make it ourselves.

So, what can you make? Do you need printables for centers that help students practice long vowel sounds? Do you need a more comprehensive assessment for your weather unit? Do you need an essay-writing unit that teaches how to write an introduction and thesis statement? Do you wish you had more examples of geometry anchor charts to capture thinking about right triangles and parallel lines? Remember, if it's a need you have or something you really excel at, chances are someone else needs it. It's okay to bottle up your ideas and share them with the world.

Let's say you're thinking, "But LaNesha and Naomi, I do have some ideas, I just don't know how to make anything." Let us stop you right there. If you are reading this book, we are willing to bet you have access to the internet or other books too. Are we right? Sounds like your imposter syndrome is creeping up, trying to talk you out of going for it.

Cue the *Hamilton* soundtrack: look around; how lucky we are to be alive right now with Google at our fingertips! Sometimes, all you need is the right phrase and you can learn to do pretty much anything. How many times has YouTube saved us? We've used videos and articles to help us with anything from repairing a broken refrigerator handle to segmenting subscribers on an email list provider. This day and age has made creating possible for just about anyone who can access the internet.

TIPS FOR GETTING STARTED

- **Done is better than perfect.** Get started. Play around. See what happens. If you sit around and fail to get started because you haven't figured out every single little thing. . .it'll never happen. Jump in and try. You'll slowly learn along the way.

- **Expect a learning curve.** If you are brand-new to this, it's likely going to cause multiple points of frustration. It's only hard until it isn't. Now that the technical things are more like second nature for us, we are free to get more creative and try new things. That didn't happen overnight. We spent plenty of time using the same template over and over because we figured out how to make it work.

- **Challenge yourself.** We've got to tell you about an exercise that we used to love to do when we started creating. We thought about it like a challenge. Now please understand that this challenge is for *you* and only *you*. When we first got started, we would see something that was really inspiring. It may have been a website, a product resource cover, or a worksheet. *For practice purposes only*, we would see if we could figure out how to recreate it. So, if we noticed that the worksheet had a border, we

> **Helpful Search Engine Terms***
> *How to Create a Resource in PowerPoint*
> *How to Turn a PowerPoint into a PDF*
> *Creative Commons Licenses*
> *Commercial Use Clip Art/Fonts/*
> *Stock Photos for Commercial Use*
>
> *Any direct feature can also be searched (i.e., how to insert a picture into PowerPoint).

would try to locate a cool border or create our own. If they placed clip art in a certain area, we would play around with placing clip art in different areas. If we noticed that the letters had a cool drop-shadow feature, we set off to teach ourselves how they did that. These documents obviously never saw the light of day. What this little exercise does is gives you the ability to learn some new tricks and design strategies. Then you can take those new tricks and use them to create *your own* style.

Okay, so we've given you all of our tips and tricks. The rest is up to you. We want to ask one final time: "What's your thing? How do you want to present it to educators or students? What is going to make your idea stand out above the rest?"

Go for it! Start right now.

Chapter 4
Online Learning: Developing Courses, Memberships, and Teaching Sessions

"You need to turn that into a course" our friend Nicole said while listening to us describe a resource that we'd created. "A what?" we thought. Nicole Turner of Simply Coaching & Teaching—a full-time instructional coach who had single handedly created the first virtual online summit for coaches—was about to rock my world with some new ideas. Part of the reason we decided to write this book is because a lot of times, you just don't know what you don't know. I had *no clue* that people could create their own courses and/or memberships. We only saw people creating resources that could be downloaded and that's it, so that's the only thing that we knew to be possible. Nicole, who is our dear friend today, showed us that we could take the knowledge and the resources that we'd been accumulating and simply put it in a certain framework that made it accessible to people in lesson-sized chunks. If you already knew this, then we're sure you're currently scoffing at our ignorance, but we truly had no idea.

Working under the assumption that this is a newer idea to you, let's break it down a bit.

ONLINE COURSES

So you have the ability to take a topic that you specialize in (literally *anything)* and turn it into an online learning experience that closely resembles a collegiate online course. Courses are typically hosted on a platform that makes it incredibly easy to create a polished and professional-looking learning experience for anyone wanting to learn from you. Our favorites include Kajabi and Thinkific, but there are plenty to choose from. You can get as fancy or simple as you'd like. Some course creators select specific colors, fonts, and branding images to use for all of the visual aspects of the course, but lots of people keep it simple and just use the features included on the platform. I'll take a minute to paint the picture of what a course might look like.

When you sign up for a course, you become a member of that course. You log in, and the first thing you might see is a welcome video recorded by the author of the course. This is where you will see the creator explain how to navigate the course and where to go if you need help. Somewhere on the screen, you see a list of videos that will probably be organized into modules or overarching topics. It will be very clearly laid out and easy to access (if it's a well-organized course). Many times, there will be specific items that will be listed alongside those videos that support the content that is in that video. Oftentimes, a course creator will create a workbook or note-taking file to accompany the videos. This will ensure that your members (the educators who signed up) are following along and taking in everything that you've designed. Courses can be as long or as short as you'd like them to be. We have seen courses with lots of videos, but the videos last anywhere from 3 to 9 minutes. We've seen other courses with only a handful of videos, but those videos can last 45 minutes to an hour. It's all about how you want to design it.

Now, we'll be honest; there are some technology tricks to learn. This is where you've got to decide to pull on that "I can do anything" attitude and figure it out. We largely figured out how to do these courses through YouTube tutorials and lots and lots of trial and error. We aren't super-"techy" so we truly believe that if we can figure it out, you most likely can too. Alternatively, if you wanted to invest, there are people who will set up your entire online course for you. They'll design it, get everything connected, and you'd be all set. We couldn't afford that our first time, so we had to attach the "YouTube Taught Me" badges firmly on our shirts. Was it perfect? *Nah*. Did we get better with time? For sure. We feel like a recurring theme in this book is "You've gotta start somewhere."

You can even offer professional development (PD) credit hours for your students, but you will want to make sure that they understand that it will be *their* responsibility to make sure that that certificate can actually count toward their hours as you likely won't be accredited.

Courses have been so powerful because you can record your videos as if you were sitting in the same room as a group of teachers and holding their hand through your topic. You may be thinking, "What would I even write a course about?" Remember what we said earlier? *Anything*. You can do academic or nonacademic topics! We've had friends offer courses on so many topics; here are a few off the top of our heads:

- How to Balance Your Teacher Workload and Take Care of Yourself
- Guided Reading
- Writing Workshop
- The Science of Reading

- Math Skills
- STEM Integration
- Social Emotional Learning
- Classroom Management Systems
- Healthy Eating for Educators

See? You can literally create a course around almost any topic! If you can break down the main topic into manageable learning chunks and actionable items, it can be made into a learning course. You can use this course to grow a community of like minded individuals by creating a support group on Facebook or another social platform that you prefer. That's where you can answer questions, shoot off new ideas, and learn from your members because the conversations will only improve the quality of your content!

Designing Your Course

Okay, let's get started by talking about supplies. What materials will be needed? Not much. We created an entire course using our laptop, iPhone, and PowerPoint. We didn't have a fancy camera or microphone. And then, of course, you need to research the software that would work best for you. That's it! The videos were created with our built-in QuickTime and iMovie programs. We've also had to set our cell phone on a tower of books and press "record" if we wanted to simply talk in our videos. It's all doable!

The amazing thing about creating courses is the fact that you already know how to teach, so the only thing to really figure out is the technology part! And, while that *can* be a bit of a learning curve, it's not too bad with the way the platforms are set up with templates that can just be edited and personalized. We also want to point out the fact that there are tons of books and courses (yes, you can take a course on *how to create a course*) and while those are great, they aren't required. We decided to glean what we could from the platform and a few Google searches, and gave it our best shot. But again, over time, we've learned new tricks and tips that have been instrumental in creating a more attractive and comprehensive experience, but we can say with certainty that we would not have ever made it to this point if we tried to learn everything there is to know about courses before launching them.

Keep it simple. If you want to create a course, get a sheet of paper and write the overarching topic. Then, list the major components that you would want to break down. It's almost like creating the title of a book and then listing out the chapters. Once you have those "chapters" created, go through and make a bulleted list of everything that you would want to include. I actually like to do this with sticky notes (in bright colors, of course). Follow this exact procedure, but jot down each "chapter" title and pop it up on the wall. You'll place the chapters' topics along the wall horizontally so that they are beside one another. From there, add the sticky notes with the ideas that are specific to that chapter and start placing them under that topic. When you're done, take a step back and look at your course. You'll see a wall covered in one big topic that has been broken down into specific topics, and each one of those topics will be developed with the key points that you choose to include. Actually, let's try it now. Here we go:

Big Idea: _____

Topic:	Topic:	Topic:	Topic:	Topic:

Major Points to include:	Major Points to include:	Major Points to include:	Major Points to include:	Major Points to include:

We know how helpful an example is for us, so here is one to consult so you can see where we're headed:

Big Idea: Math Workshop

Topic:	Topic:	Topic:	Topic:	Topic:
Setting the stage for success: Math Management	Number Sense Routines	Manipulatives	Assessment and Enrichment	Logistics (schedules, tips, tricks, etc.)

Major Points to include:	Major Points to include:	Major Points to include:	Major Points to include:	Major Points to include:
Partner structures Math Conversation starters Becoming mathe-maticians (identity work)	Share my warm-up routine Teach each math game and include printable directions	How to organize materials Alternatives for materials My individual student math kits	Using math notebooks Problem-solving challenges Remedia-tion tools at the ready	Share mul-tiple math block sched-ules based on time How to organize students for learning Tips for max-imizing math minutes

So, this may not look like it, but this is a course. It is! From here, you would begin to take this information and create some slides that flesh out each point. You would use these slides (we like to use PowerPoint or Canva to create slides) to do a voice over recording so that you can actually teach your course members what's on the slide. You can also use programs like Loom or Screencastify that will allow your face to be present in the corner of the screen if you choose.

Crafting Your Slides

Let's stick with the math example. The first topic is your first module, so for this example, Module One is all about managing the classroom for a successful math workshop. The major points are (1) partner structures, (2) Math Conversation starters, and (3) becoming mathematicians (identity work). When creating the slides, you probably will want to include some clip art or fonts that you like (we point out some logistics for this in Chapter 3 about creating resources) so that the slides look professional and polished. From there, you can include bullet points, quotes, or other things that will trigger what you want to say on the video. Try to refrain from putting tons of words on the screen. People have short attention spans, and it can be more effective

Figure 4.1 Scenes from a reading course for teachers.

to spread your knowledge across multiple slides instead of having a really wordy slide that you'll talk from for 10 minutes. Figure 4.1 shows some examples from a reading course that we created. Notice the clip art, the fonts, and the stock photos.

You can include photos, videos, and other examples of what you are talking about. We've included photos from our learning spaces that showcase exactly what we are talking about. If you are ever going to use examples of student work, *always* get written permission from their guardians and make sure they understand exactly how you plan to use it. Photos and videos can be really powerful because the proof is undeniable. If you are creating a resource around a topic that you are passionate about and you fully believe other educators can be successful, you're going to want to make the process so easy and seamless that they walk away from your lesson ready to implement what they just learned.

This brings us to a critical part of the equation: actionable items. You want your course to be full of what a lot of people refer to as "quick wins." After giving your members a lesson, you want to give them "homework." But this homework should be quick and easy to implement. This will make your members feel like they are well on their way to mastering the content. If you're not sure about what to assign, it can be anything from (sticking with our math example) filling out your course outline for this module and thinking through how you will reorganize your math tubs to "Go into your classroom and organize your math tools as we discussed in this lesson." We like to assign two or three quick tasks at the end of each lesson, depending on the length of the video. If you are creating videos that are super-quick (less than 5 minutes), then you probably wouldn't assign an actionable item. We like to keep our lesson videos around the 10–15-minute mark, because it can make it much more manageable for our members.

When it comes to creating a course, think about how you would make your lessons engaging for students. You want to deliver your lessons in a way that is a bit fun, exciting, or interesting so that they will actually want to pay attention and learn. Teachers are no different. No one wants to listen to another teacher go on and on about their idea in a flat monotonous tone with boring slides. Don't be afraid to record with energy, use some humor, and pick a few colors to brand your course with so that it looks like something that people will want to listen to.

Branding Your Course

You don't *have* to do this, but it's so nice when you sign into a course and the branding is connected and beautiful. When we say *branding* we simply mean creating a distinctive design for your course (Figure 4.2). We try to keep it simple by selecting no more than three fonts (one cursive-ish, one bold, and one thin) and a palette of colors to work with. Here are a few tricks we love to Google:

1. Google the term *font pairing guide* and study how people pair fonts together. You'll start to develop a sense of fonts that clash or fit together beautifully. From there, you can find similar fonts that are free for commercial use or you can purchase them if you really want a particular one. Remember, fonts need to be accessible. If it's too hard to read, it can frustrate your members. Simple and clean fonts are safe.

2. Google the term *pallette picker* and check out the links that come up! Some of the websites will show you a host of color pallets that have already been created. You can click through them until you land on a pallet that has a handful of colors that you enjoy. From there, you'll note the hex code (which is just a created code that identifies shades

Figure 4.2 Reading course logo.

of colors on the web) and those codes can be entered on a website like Canva so that you get the exact colors that you wanted. If you design on PowerPoint, you could copy and paste your palette into the document and then use the eyedropper tool to match the colors. Those are the colors that you'll use for everything you create!

3. Google *free icons for commercial use* and find yourself a clip art image that you can use with your branding. If you notice, we decided to use an image of a child reading to accompany our course branding items. You'll see a fun font, thick font, clip art, and two or three colors that we selected for our course. Done! All of this was created in PowerPoint. It's doable!

Spreading the Word

You're probably thinking, "Say I go ahead and create this course. . .how would I even get people to sign up for it?" Valid question. We have a few ideas. Obviously, the advice that we mention in Chapter 1 on social media applies for sure. Making sure you begin to position yourself as an expert in this topic will certainly be the place that you'd want to begin sharing your knowledge on your topic. But another strategy that can have a huge impact is collecting emails. There are tons of ways that you can collect emails but one sure fire strategy is to create a product that goes with your course that you can offer to people for free. You'll want this resource to be enticing enough to where people will think, "I can't believe they are giving this away for free. If this free resource is this good, then the course must be amazing!"

But at the same time, you don't want to give away everything for free because, well, the name of the game is to bring in income while helping educators. There are a lot of fun and catchy strategies for creating free resources. You can create an ebook using the strategies that we include in Chapter 3 about creating and selling resources. For example, if we were creating that course about the math workshop, we could create an ebook and title it "*5 Ways to Set Up a Math Workshop that Will Run Itself!*" Inside the ebook, you could include photographs, tips, and ideas that would be very helpful to an educator. A helpful mantra to remember goes "Tell *what* but not *how*" in a free resource like this. You could create a bundle of free worksheets, checklists, or guides that will make an educator think "I have to have this!" It's your chance to show off how knowledgeable you are. Crafting a really great freebie is a way to give your potential members a taste of what they will be getting if they join your course. Your expertise is worth paying for, especially if you have poured hours into what you are putting back out into the world.

Marketing Your Course

So, how does the free resource connect with the course? Email! We are going to try to simplify a very complex topic in the next few paragraphs. Email marketing can be intense, but it can also be a simple and streamlined process. The first thing you want to do is select an email service provider. Some of them are free until you reach a certain number of subscribers and then they will ask you to pay. Some platforms are more expensive than others and that is often due to the capabilities on each platform. At the end of the day, you just want to be able to collect emails.

When we first started, we chose what was cheap and easy to use. Eventually, as we learned more, we started to experiment with different email service providers. One of the functions that many email providers will give you is the ability to create a form. You may have seen this before. You have probably seen a free resource that you wanted to have and you thought to yourself, "That looks great! It's free. . .all I have to do is click this button!" But, instead of the resource coming directly to you, you were taken to another screen and asked to enter your email address. If this has ever happened to you, then you were a part of an email marketing strategy. You got an incredible free resource, and in turn, they got your email address to let you know about future projects or resources they'll be showcasing. What you have done is given your email to this person and you will likely be signed up for subsequent emails afterward. The page that asks you to enter your email address is a form or a landing page.

It sounds way more involved than it really is. Your email provider will walk you through the setup. Essentially, you would design your form or landing page with whatever colors and images you want, and include the link to the free resource that you created. You can upload a free resource directly or you can have it in a Google folder, for example (or Dropbox. . .or any other service provider), and that is what people would get once they entered their email address. Once you design your landing page, you will get a link that is shareable or can even be embedded on your website using a code. Whenever you decide to post your free resource, you would just tell people to click that link that you created in your email service and people would give you their email in exchange for your resource. You must disclose that they are joining your email list (you'll typically have that wording included when you set up your account with your email service provider) so that people are aware that they are signing up to get emails from you. We never want anyone to feel tricked or scammed. That's not the point of any of this. If you are someone who is going to be helpful, people are going to want to hear from you.

Once they have received that free resource, you can set up what is called a funnel, or a sequence. That simply means that you will prewrite a series of emails, maybe four or five emails that will be delivered one after the other. That means anytime somebody signs up to get your free resource they would enter a funnel sequence where you can leave them some bread crumbs to get them to arrive at your course. The following is an example of a four-email sequence that could be sent out. Each email might say something like:

Email 1: Welcome! I'm so glad to have you as a part of this list. I hope you enjoy your freebie, and we will talk soon!

Email 2: How did that freebie go? Did you enjoy it? Reply back and let me know!

Email 3: Are you ready to take your Math Workshop to the next level? Here's one more tip that I wanted to send your way. (Provide a tip. You're making yourself the "expert" here; they are starting to believe that you are the go-to person for your topic.)

Email 4: What if I told you I could help you implement a Math Workshop that will essentially run itself? I can! Let me introduce you to my passion project. . .(explain the course).

So as you can see, in four emails I have introduced myself, given a freebie, added some value to help educators who are looking for more tips to use in their classrooms, and then mentioned that there is a course out there that can help them if they have enjoyed the content that they have received from me thus far. Each one of those emails can be spaced apart as far as you would like them to be. We typically like to space emails at least a week apart because nobody likes to feel harassed by daily emails. Now obviously all of those emails would be much more thought out and intentional, but you can see the gist in those previous sentences. The beautiful thing about this is that you sit down and create all of those emails at once. After that point, you don't ever really have to bother with them again! But every time you share that free resource that you created, someone will enter their email address, and without you doing any more work, they will be signed up to get the next set of emails in that sequence.

Now we will be honest and say that there is a ton more to learn about email marketing, but remember this book is your starting point. It's a launch pad. This is a place where we can walk you through the big picture, but it's going to be up to you to figure it out. Also, keep in mind that the strategies listed here about marketing courses can be adjusted and applied to all of the concepts in the other chapters as well.

A little word of wisdom on courses: if this chapter isn't resonating with you at this point, don't count it out! You might find that the chapter about creating resources is more your speed and that's great. But once you have a handful of products under your belt you might stop and ask yourself, "What else can I do with this?" That's where something like a course will come in handy! You'll be able to take those resources or the framework that you created and expand it so that educators can access it in a different way.

Pricing Your Course

When you've jumped into course creation, you'll pour hours and hours into building it. That may make you think, "This took me so long, I'm charging a billion dollars!" But, you have to reframe your thinking, especially in the world of education. In other industries, we have seen people create courses and charge people up to $10,000! After picking our jaws up off the floor, we had to start researching to see what an appropriate rate would be for the kind of work we were putting out. Not only that, but if you recall in Chapter 3 about creating resources, we mention that you don't necessarily bake in the price of the items that you used to create the resource, but you charge for the final product that the individual will be walking away with. Courses are similar.

There's a delicate balance to charging an appropriate rate for your time and effort and keeping it affordable for a person who decided to purchase out of pocket. The best scenario (in our opinion) happens when a school will allow an educator to use funds to get access to a course because then the educator isn't out money. We've noticed that for educators, the rates will vary from $37 for a mini-course to around $197 for a full-blown course. There are naturally outliers, but that's the price bracket that we've seen. Your platform will most likely allow you to offer payment options as well. Our courses have the option to do a one-time payment or break it into three payments, for example. You will also (depending on your platform) be able to create coupon codes and promotional discounts if you'd like. How amazing is that? There are so many options out there for us to engage in to create amazing business opportunities for ourselves. It'll take some work, but just a few short years ago, this wasn't even an option (at least not with this much ease and accessibility) for the general masses. We think that's pretty cool.

The Pros and Cons of Online Courses

The Pros of Online Courses

Online courses are great because you truly get to break your content down into manageable chunks that are more easily digested. Unlike a PD session or speech where you participate briefly in a workshop, you can really give your students a comprehensive understanding of the topic. Many people enjoy the fact that a course can be self-paced (though not all are) because they are able to fit it in at a time that works well for them.

The Cons of Online Courses

There's a lot of work up front! You will want to create an experience that is organized and efficient for your students—especially if your students are busy educators. Also, there will more than likely be some upfront costs involved (paying for the platform, e.g.); it is a bit of an investment.

COURSE MEMBERSHIPS

Another option that is similar to an online course is creating what is called a membership. Our friend, Brittany Hege (membership extraordinaire) of Mix and Math, introduced us to the world of memberships and helped us launch our first social studies membership. She helped us form a conceptual understanding about how memberships can work. As she explained to us, a membership is similar to a course, but instead of a one-time payment, there is a lower monthly payment. Think: Netflix, but for educators! Really, you can think of any subscription service and apply the concept here. Netflix is an open library that you can access anywhere, anytime, right? You pay a monthly fee and you get access. There are also services like Ipsy, a monthly makeup subscription bag that comes with a new variety of items each month. Your membership could be modeled in the same way!

Imagine logging into a membership and seeing a collection of videos. You can click any of the videos at any time to watch the course creator explain a concept and then give you all of the tools that you need in order to execute it. That's the idea! In a membership, you can upload short training videos in which you can explain an idea, strategy, activity. . .or anything else that you can think of. Then, you can include the accompanying resources as downloads that would be needed in order to execute that idea or strategy.

For example, let's go back to our math example. If we wanted to create a math membership, we would create a series of videos in which we would show members a particular strategy or math game that is really effective in the classroom. Then we could end the video by saying, "If you are ready to try this out with your students, make sure you check the downloads below this video, print them out, and you should be good to go!" It is like a guided experience for people who want to get some support for their daily instruction.

So, if memberships are more like a subscription service, you are going to be offering lots of resources or ideas/activities on a monthly basis. There are so many ways you can do this. You can choose to take a bunch of activities and upload them to the course, and people can pay to have access to the resources whenever they would like. You could also choose to withhold the content and drip it to your members. That means that certain content would be locked until a specific date. Naturally, there are pros and cons to all of these options. For example, some pros include creating a community of educators who believe in and find value in your work, giving educators access to a large body of work for a smaller monthly fee, and the fact that once you upload the resource and/or video, you're done. Some cons include the fact that someone really could choose to subscribe for a month, download everything, and then cancel the subscription. There are ways to discourage that and make it a more tedious task, but it can be done.

We have been creating resources together since 2015. That means that there are tons and tons of resources in our online stores. We were asking ourselves how we could diversify the methods in which we made those resources available and that's where the idea of memberships came in. With some help, we decided to upload all of our resources (and we are talking hundreds of resources) to a platform call Kajabi. We decided that we would make our entire library of resources available to anyone who wanted to become a subscriber. Currently, for under $15 a month, our subscribers have access to *all* of those resources. We organized them by months, themes, and any other category that made sense. We could have stopped there because that subscription pays for itself with just a few downloads, but we wanted to make it more of a PD experience for teachers who were looking for support around the area of social studies.

We decided that we would upload what we like to call "Pop-In PD" videos every month. That means that if there is a particular topic coming up, like a holiday or a historical event where teachers might want some support in teaching that content honestly and inclusively, our videos would support that. We also have a question box where our members can drop questions that they have. We take those questions and we create a "You Asked, We Answered" video at the first of the month. It's like a rapid-fire Q & A session where questions get answered in a discussion-style format. We simply hop on a Zoom meeting and have a conversation about the questions that were asked, and then we upload the recording for our members to view. It's a really great way to build community and have our members feel as though they are being supported with content that they may not feel confident teaching. We're doing this work from

Indianapolis and Los Angeles because of the amazing platforms that are available to us. The sky is truly the limit!

The Pros of Memberships

Memberships can provide a more consistent stream of income. Once you're up and running (and depending on how you might structure a membership), memberships don't have to be a high-commitment obligation if you don't want them to be. You can be as involved as you'd like to be.

The Cons of Memberships

There's a lot of work up front, so you'll need to be prepared to buckle down and get it done. You also have to make sure you have a plan to retain your members. You may have to get creative with how you add value so that members feel the need to continue paying their monthly fee.

LIVE AND PRERECORDED TEACHING

We wanted to share a few more experiences that we have had with online learning. Using the same platforms (mostly Kajabi and Hey Summit), we decided to host camps for children over the summer! Naomi created a prerecorded experience (that we will get into in the following) and LaNesha created a writing camp where she showed up live to instruct children all over the world during a four-week camp. (More information about virtual camps is given later.)

LaNesha's Live Camp

Here's how it worked. I used the platform that I host my courses on to create a new product (Figure 4.3). I got on my personal Facebook page and all of my social media platforms, and I told

Figure 4.3 Virtual summer camp ad example.

everybody that I was going to be teaching live writing lessons for the summer. I laid out the experience for them. I told them that we would meet three times a week and I would turn their children into little authors in just four weeks. I actually got my own two children on board. (I paid them for their time, don't worry!) But for four weeks they showed up with me and co-taught writing lessons as children from all over the globe looked on and participated with us.

I designed the lessons so that the students would be able to master the writing process and create pieces of writing alongside us. It was epic! Again, pros and cons. . . . For me, showing up live was honestly exhausting. I was only doing 30-minute sessions, but that meant that I needed to be camera-ready and have my children in the right mood in order to get this done. But a lot of the families really appreciated the live interaction. We would, of course, record all of the meetings and upload them so that children who weren't able to attend live for whatever reason would have access to the videos and could catch up. I did leave myself the ability to prerecord a lesson or two because of my traveling schedule so that was definitely helpful.

Hopefully you are reading this and thinking about the ways you could put together something like this! Parents are looking for enrichment or remediation opportunities all of the time. What topic are you really good at? What are the skills that your students master year after year? You can take that content, map out a four-week sequence of lessons, and show up live to teach those lessons to the students who sign up. I also created a parent guide that would help parents or guardians to be able to get on board with what I was going to be teaching. This was really helpful! It was that front-loading that allowed for the students to be successful because the parents or guardians knew how to support their child with the lessons that they would be getting from me. If you are looking for a summer hustle, you can teach the summer school sessions at your district or you could literally create your own summer school experience. Reach out to your personal network; you probably know a ton of people who have children who would love to learn from you!

The Pros of Live Teaching

For me, the pros are being able to see real, live students daily. That was everything! I could also work in real time and didn't have to have everything done in advance. I would have a teaching point for that day and then show up and do it. Easy!

The Cons of Live Teaching

Going live every day quickly became exhausting. It was also difficult because I felt tethered to my computer for two months. That made traveling while doing these sessions tricky as well.

Naomi's Prerecorded Camp

Even though my Instagram account was a place for me to share ideas for K–2 educators, it slowly also became a place for me to share my ideas and insights about teaching children to be anti-racist. Remember how we talked about establishing yourself as the authority? Well, I was the authority when it came to talking to young children about bias, stereotypes, identity, and diversity. I created posts, videos with my son, and resources, but caregivers and educators were still needing a bit more. I found myself overwhelmed with direct messages (DMs), but many were asking the same questions. I decided to host an online summer camp to help adults support children in their lives in this area. Using the platform HeySummit and trusty old PowerPoint, I created images and outlined what my summer course would offer (Figure 4.4). I created a calendar and planned a 20-day virtual summer camp. (See Figure 4.5.)

Using resources I already created, I recorded videos guiding attendees through my lessons with my son. I incorporated frequently asked questions and addressed concerns many caregivers had been expressing. Because it was prerecorded, people could tune in at a time that was convenient for them and their children.

So for my online course, attendees received a bundle of my resources, including an exclusive unit that hadn't been released yet. They got daily videos to help navigate each lesson, and they were given access to a private Facebook group for the duration of the online camp. Attendees could ask questions, share their learning and work, and build a community with one another.

Figure 4.4 Virtual summer camp ad example.

The Pros of Prerecorded Teaching

The pros for me were that once it was done, it was done! The videos were uploaded, the resources had been emailed, and I felt confident in the content my son and I were sharing.

The Cons of Prerecorded Teaching

The cons were staying on schedule to get all of the videos recorded and edited or re-filmed ahead of time. I wanted to

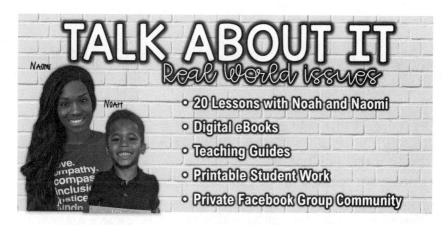

Figure 4.5 Virtual summer camp ad example.

make sure the lighting and sound quality were always good, so that meant that I only had small windows during the day to film. Filming, and then rewatching each video was time-consuming.

All in all, it was well worth it: 5 out of 5 stars. Would recommend.

TIPS FOR GETTING STARTED

As you can see, the online learning possibilities are limitless! There's so many variations that can be put together to bring in some extra income. Some of them can be longer projects that last for years (like courses and memberships) and other ones can be short-term, one-time experiences (like a summer online camp). You can even offer virtual tutoring in small groups. We've seen people create summer camps around sports, crafts, book clubs, and more. You likely have the idea; you just need to figure out how to package it and make it accessible to people! Map out your content in manageable chunks and figure out what downloadable resources you can offer to support your lessons.

Finally, if you're at the end of the chapter thinking that there's no way you are ready for this or that "you could never. . .," open your calendar—digital or paper—right now. One year from today, create an appointment and tell yourself to reread this chapter. Your eyes will have a new lens. It's like when you buy a new car and suddenly you notice that car everywhere. You'll notice more courses and membership opportunities as you scroll through social media or check your email. Things will begin to seem more feasible the more you watch other people do it. You never know, this time next year you might be primed and ready to dive in! You owe it to yourself to circle back and reconsider.

- Fill out the graphic organizer in this chapter. Get your plan in order so that when it's time to put it together you have a clear path for content.

- Begin researching platforms for online learning. Actually, Google "platforms for online learning or course" and do your homework! Compare pricing plans, features, and ease of use. Watch a few YouTube videos from people who use these platforms (there are tons) and make the decision that will best suit your needs.

- Look for some examples of other courses from educators so that you can get a feel for how courses can be branded. As always, be inspired but never copy. You can also use that opportunity to notice how those course are priced.

- Work on finding an email platform that will allow you to collect some emails and create an automated sequence of emails. This will save you tons of time when it's time to com-municate with your members. *Note: Many online learning platforms actually include an email service that you can use to create some funnels, so be sure to look out for that option!*

Chapter 5
Virtual Services

At this point we are confident that we've given you something you can take and run with to make edupreneurship happen for you. But, if we haven't, don't worry. We still have a few more amazing ideas to run by you.

Okay, let's go back to that coffee shop we met up at in the Introduction of this book. How are you now? What have you been brainstorming for yourself and your potential business? You're still feeling a little lost? That's okay, bestie. We want to talk to you about virtual services.

So maybe the thought of maintaining a social media account, creating resources, public speaking, selling merch, running a membership, or filming a course didn't sound appealing to you. That's okay. It's good to know what you don't like. If you're pushing yourself to do something that's *way* out of your comfort zone, it might not work out for you. We said *way* for a reason. Sometimes we can grow from discomfort. For us, some of the biggest jumps we took with our businesses came from places of discomfort and being unsure. We have been very transparent about our journeys, so you have been able to see that for most of these ventures, it was something we never thought we'd be doing, but we are very grateful that we did. So, even if some things aren't a fit for you right now, it doesn't mean that you can't work it in later. Let these ideas marinate in your mind for a while before giving a hard "no."

Virtual services may be the thing for you, though. When we say *virtual services*, we mean the act of working with or for someone who is not physically in your presence. Your primary means of communicating will be through direct messages (DM) online, over the phone, or through email. Virtual services can also be something that you do virtually using your skills or educational background. The evolution of the way the internet is used these days has allowed more people to have access to business opportunities that they would have never had before. Google and YouTube or the right book can teach us virtually anything we need to know (pun intended).

TUTORING OR TEACHING VIRTUAL SUMMER SCHOOL

The most obvious service to offer virtually is tutoring or teaching summer school. Now, the thought of teaching summer school can bring out many emotions in a group of educators. Some educators loathe it, but need the money; some educators avoid it all costs; and some educators look forward to the extra money and don't mind spending their time teaching over the summer. Whatever your feelings toward summer school are, what if we told you that you could run your own summer school from the comfort of your own living quarters?

Using a platform like Zoom, you can host your own virtual summer school or one-on-one tutoring sessions. You can reach out to caregivers in your school community, neighborhood, or online to gauge interest in what you have to offer.

Let's say that you are a great reading, writing, science, or math teacher. You can choose one of those subjects and offer your services to support kids who need to strengthen those areas over the summer. Make sure to be as specific as possible so that people signing up for your summer school course know what they're getting. Is it for kindergarten students who are struggling to decode words? Is it for third graders who need work with fractions over the summer? Is it a science club where students will be able to investigate and conduct experiments? Be specific!

Virtual Event Ideas

What can you offer that can be taught on an online platform?

How many children do you think you can manage virtually?

How long will your event run?

What will you charge per family?

Early Bird Rate:

Regular Rate:

Will any printables be needed?

How will you advertise for your virtual event?

The Pros and Cons of Tutoring or Teaching Virtual Summer School

The Pros

When you're doing things virtually, you can do them from the comfort of your own home and you can make your own schedule. You get to decide if lessons will be live or prerecorded, and you can work with students virtually anywhere (again, pun intended).

The Cons

Virtually teaching and tutoring can be tricky if you don't feel like you're able to engage with your clients on a personal level. Technology can sometimes be a problem as well. Ensuring that you use secure platforms and that your internet isn't having any issues is a must.

OFFERING VIRTUAL SERVICES

Another path you can explore is becoming a virtual assistant (VA) to other business owners. Some educators who are running businesses are constantly looking for other educators to work with them and help them manage it all. From writing blog posts to editing resources to answering emails, there are so many virtual jobs you can apply for. We can personally attest to the power of hiring a VA who is or was also an educator. There is just a level of knowledge that comes with other educators that we don't have to teach because they just know due to their backgrounds.

Some educators are looking for ghostwriters. Ghostwriters can write content for emails, blog posts, and even social media posts. If you have a way with words and a couple of hours to spare, this could be the job for you. You will have to work out the logistics of how sharing passwords will work. Some people just straight-up share their logins and passwords, and other people use options like LastPass.

We have seen some VAs charge by the task or charge by the hour. We personally like being able to purchase packages of virtual assistance by the hour. For example, we have worked with virtual assistants who offer 5, 10, or 20 hours of work. We are able to purchase the amount of hours that work for upcoming projects we have and everyone wins.

Whether you are looking for a VA or hoping to become one, we believe that a good contract can go a long way. It's important for you to set a vision for your VA business and let people know what to expect from you. In figure 5.1 you can see Naomi's company vision, mission, and breakdown of some of the things she has going on.

After being inspired by *New York Times* best-selling author and speaker Luvvie Ajayi, we took the time to write down our own core values visions for our companies that we slowly grew into.

More Virtual Work Ideas

- <u>Email Management</u>: Replying to questions, unsubscribing from unwanted lists, forwarding messages, drafting responses, following up on emails sent, transcribing emails, setting up appointments, adding meetings to calendar, drafting emails, managing calendar, managing files

- <u>Resource Management</u>: Uploading resources, updating resources, writing product descriptions, researching resource content, creating templates, editing resources

- <u>Personal Tasks</u>: Creating grocery lists, booking appointments, paying bills, researching and booking travel arrangements, assisting with event planning, making wake-up calls, sending reminder texts of important events, preparing schedules

- <u>Bookkeeping</u>: Processing payments, managing affiliate payouts, providing basic payroll duties, creating and sending invoices, billing, compiling profit-and-loss statements

- <u>Customer Service</u>: Following up on orders, responding to feedback, handling customer inquiries and complaints, processing orders, following up with payments

- <u>Social Media Management</u>: Creating posting schedule, sending reminders about posts, creating in-feed posts, researching trends, supporting business with branding, interacting with followers, monitoring hashtags, developing campaigns, analyzing insights, seeking brand sponsorships, hosting giveaways

We always refer to them when making business moves. This is something that we incorporate into the contracts of the people whom we work with or people who work for us.

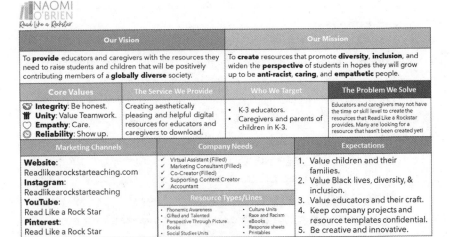

Our Vision		Our Mission	
To **provide** educators and caregivers with the resources they need to raise students and children that will be positively contributing members of a **globally diverse** society.		To **create** resources that promote **diversity**, **inclusion**, and widen the **perspective** of students in hopes they will grow up to be **anti-racist**, **caring**, and **empathetic** people.	

Core Values	The Service We Provide	Who We Target	The Problem We Solve
⚓ **Integrity**: Be honest. 🏆 **Unity**: Value Teamwork. ♡ **Empathy**: Care. 🕐 **Reliability**: Show up.	Creating aesthetically pleasing and helpful digital resources for educators and caregivers to download.	• K-3 educators. • Caregivers and parents of children in K-3.	Educators and caregivers may not have the time or skill level to create the resources that Read Like a Rockstar provides. Many are looking for a resource that hasn't been created yet!

Marketing Channels	Company Needs		Expectations
Website: Readlikearockstarteaching.com **Instagram:** Readlikearockstarteaching **YouTube:** Read Like a Rock Star **Pinterest:** Read Like a Rock Star	✓ Virtual Assistant (Filled) ✓ Marketing Consultant (Filled) ✓ Co-Creator (Filled) ✓ Supporting Content Creator ✓ Accountant		1. Value children and their families. 2. Value Black lives, diversity, & inclusion. 3. Value educators and their craft. 4. Keep company projects and resource templates confidential. 5. Be creative and innovative.
	Resource Types/Lines		
	• Phonemic Awareness • Gifted and Talented • Perspective Through Picture Books • Social Studies Units	• Culture Units • Race and Racism • eBooks • Response sheets • Printables	

Figure 5.1 Virtual summer camp ad example.

Consider creating something similar for yourself. You may find yourself going back to add to it from time to time as your new business ventures grow and change over time. When you are deciding whether or not to work with someone, you can make sure that your core values and visions align.

Before you jump into just any old virtual job, make sure it's a great fit and partnership. Do you support the content they are producing? Does it align with your beliefs or morals?

Do you all have work styles and communication styles that will be compatible so that both parties will be satisfied and can maintain a professional work relationship?

Consider setting up an initial call to make sure you can meet all of a potential client's needs.

LaNesha's Virtual Services Journey

Honestly, my journey has been short. The thing is, to use VAs, you have to have a lot of faith and trust. It's really about finding a good match. I hired someone to help me manage emails, but

I quickly found that to be frustrating because while I needed help, I couldn't keep my nosey self out of my email inbox. So, I'd find myself talking to my VA and I'd already know everything that she was going to say because I'd read the emails. I hired another person to do some blogging for me, but something was just. . .missing. I finally connected with a teacher who uses my products in her classroom and knew them really well. I randomly asked her if she was interested in making some extra cash to write about what she's already doing in her class with my resources. She said "yes," and it's been a match made in heaven. She's proactive, constantly coming to me with ideas (so that takes some of the burden off of me), and she's super-eager to learn. I set up a few training videos to show her my process for blogging and now she's contracted out with me for a certain amount of hours per month. I also gave her full access to every resource I created, so she is able to use whatever she needs. This connection gave me hope, but while VAs were seemingly falling into Naomi's lap (as you'll read shortly) I, the one who introduced the concept to her, couldn't get the help I needed for the longest time!

I eventually made my second hire who has saved me a ton of time. I have resources on multiple (three, actually) websites available for purchase. That's cool until you realize that a resource has a typo or needs to be updated. Then, it's a nightmare! You have to locate the resource, make the correction, save it in the right format, go to each website's back-end, replace the file, and notify buyers that it's been updated. It's a lot, and it's *very* easy to miss a step. I decided I needed a resource manager who knew my products as well as I did. I was looking to train someone who could take that initiative and email *me* to say something like, "Hey, I noticed that your spelling resource doesn't have a preview" or "The product description on this resource could be stronger, I'll tweak it."

I found someone and spent a good amount of time training her on how to do those tasks that sucked my motivation right out of me. Now, if something needs to be updated or uploaded, I send it to her and she handles it from start to finish. Best hiring decision ever. Again, she only works a certain amount of hours for me a month because I have to budget as well, but she knows that she can count on that extra income each month by helping me out.

Naomi's Virtual Services Journey

I personally have worked with a handful of people virtually. Some of the collaborations have been amazing, and some experiences I could have done without.

My most wonderful virtual partnership has been with LaNesha Tabb. When she reached out to me years ago to collaborate on some social studies resources, I had no idea I'd be gaining a best friend and creating a line of work that hundreds, if not thousands of educators would be using in their classrooms. When we first began our work we communicated solely through Facebook Messages. We would send our files back and forth and send messages about ideas all via private messages. One day, LaNesha discovered the app Marco Polo. It's a video messaging app that allows us to communicate more efficiently. We could talk to each other about what we were creating and show the tasks we were working on. We still use this app to chat every day.

Remember earlier in this book when I mentioned that during the summer of 2020 my Instagram grew to 137,000 followers? Well, my emails began blowing up as well. When things got too overwhelming to handle all on my own, I had to take at least one thing off of my plate. Lucky for me, a friend of mine whom I met online mentioned that her cousin was a VA who was looking for new clients. This was seriously a Godsend because LaNesha had been talking to me about growing a business team for a while. I felt comfortable hiring her because of the connection to my friend. It can feel hard to trust someone you've never met to go through your emails or access your calendar, but hiring a VA was a game-changer for me. She offered monthly packages and allowed me to choose the best way for us to correspond with one another. Since Marco Polo had already worked so well for LaNesha, that's the path I chose for communication. My VA checks my emails and handles what she can, but then checks in with me for emails that need me to weigh in on. She follows up on emails, adds meetings to my calendar, and really just makes sure that I know what's going on when I would otherwise be lost. For a period of time, she was also creating newsletters for my business. Another virtual service she assists me with is uploading resources to my website and sending out resources when anyone has an issue accessing them. One of the most amazing things my VA does is utilize the power of Google. Whenever I ask about something she has no idea about, she heads to Google to teach herself as much as possible. It is so appreciated when she takes that initiative to go above and beyond. It has been so helpful to me to feel like I have a teammate to help me take care of those tasks so that I can be free to focus on other tasks. I have to admit, I was resistant to the idea of hiring someone for a while because I didn't know where to even begin looking for someone, so I was thankful that this kinda fell into place so easily. She truly feels like a member of my team and helps me accomplish so much.

My last, and newest virtual service came to me through—surprise—social media! An Instagram follower turned friend reached out to me via email and inquired about helping me create resources. This was truly an answered prayer because earlier that week I'd been wanting to hire someone to help me finish up some of the many projects I'd started and I didn't know where to start looking. This virtual creator has helped both LaNesha and me get our resources and blog posts to the finish line. It was a perfect fit because she was already familiar with our work because of Instagram. So, using the Marco Polo app, we would share a vision, idea, or blog post with her and talk through the direction we wanted to take it. We would start the resource, create a template, or help plan the blog post content, and then our virtual creator would take it out of our hands and do the rest. When she was finished, she'd hand it back over to us, and we would look over it and add our finishing touches. It has been so helpful. Some people craft interview questions to find their perfect fits; this wasn't the route I took, but I definitely will in the future.

I say all of this to show what a virtual partnership could look like for you. You never know what kind of virtual help someone will need.

Now, I'm sure you remember that earlier I said there were some virtual partnerships that didn't quite work out? I'll mention those briefly as a cautionary tale, and perhaps you can pick up a thing or two about what *not* to do.

I had one virtual partnership and they had extremely poor communication. Projects were never finished on time as a result, and this partnership didn't end well and the other party was unwilling to admit that their time management and communication could be improved.

I entered into a virtual partnership with a person who over-promised and underdelivered. This person wasn't completely honest about the skills they possessed. They answered a job posting I listed on www.Upwork.com, and I had specific needs. After this person accepted the position, it became clear very quickly that they weren't going to be a good fit. I felt like both of us had our time wasted.

The Pros and Cons of Virtual Services

The Pros

Much like virtual tutoring and teaching, you can do it from the comfort of your own home. You can work with clients near and far as long as you have access to the right technology to do so.

The Cons

With communication and services being offered digitally, it can be easy to misinterpret tones and expectations. Make sure to be clear and ask for clarification often.

TIPS FOR GETTING STARTED

But, how do you get started with this work? How can you find clients? There are formal websites where you can sign up as a freelance VA and people can find you. You'll want to search phrases like "freelance service providers" or "contract work for hire," and check out those options. Essentially, you list your skills, qualities, and tasks that you're comfortable with and create a profile of sorts. From there, if someone needs an editor or a copywriter, they can search and find your page to see if it's a good match. If you're the organized, detail-oriented person who can help someone else with their business, you'll never be out of work. People will list tons of tasks that they are comfortable with but here are some examples:

- Managing emails
- Writing blog posts
- Organizing calendars
- Helping with phone calls

- Repurposing content (e.g., watching someone's YouTube video, taking notes on it, and then turning it into a blog post)
- Managing schedules
- Entering data/updating resources (e.g., using your awesome design eye to create new product covers for someone else's store)
- Providing bookkeeping services
- Fulfilling SEO (search engine optimization) tasks
- Booking travel and accommodations
- Scheduling meetings
- Performing market research
- Designing social media posts

You have no clue how much entrepreneurs need help with tasks like these! This is definitely something that you will want to get into if you already have a natural knack for organization, design, or if you're just one of those angels who finds joy in helping others. You wouldn't want to get hired by someone to create an eye-catching product cover or preview, but have no idea how to use a program like Canva or even download fonts. This kind of job works best when you take a skill set that you've already mastered, and then you offer it to other people as a service.

Another way to get into this work is simply by reaching out to an educator who seems to be juggling a lot and seeing if they (or anyone they know) are looking for someone to complete tasks for them. A lot of this work is completed via email. So, what do you think? Does this sound tailor-made for you? Take the first step: come up with a list of services you know you can provide and find someone who needs them!

Chapter 6
Becoming an Author

Before you skip over this chapter because "I could never be an author . . . "—let us stop you right there. As two people with a combined total of four books (currently, as three more books between us are on the way as we write this chapter), we can say with certainty that we *never* thought that we would ever call ourselves authors. It just wasn't in the cards. Writing books was something that bookish, serious people who had access to an elite club were allowed to do. We were just minding our own business, teaching in our classrooms until one day we started to share our ideas. Here's a snapshot of our journey.

Back in 2015, we were teaching kindergarten in Indianapolis and first grade in Denver. It was the brink of election season, and if you remember anything about that time, let's say it was . . . charged. We began to notice disturbing comments and situations (dealing with political sound bites from *children*) being reported not only on the news, but also in our own classrooms. We won't get into the specifics, but just know that a lot of the rhetoric that we were hearing in the media had trickled down to our five- and six-year-old students. The more we would share with each other, the more we realized that social studies was severely lacking in our classrooms. We started asking other educators about their social studies curriculum, and the consensus was that they either (1) weren't teaching it at all, and if they were, it was (2) outdated, biased, and honestly just false. Without going into our entire story, you should know that from there we simply started dreaming of what a social studies curriculum would look like if it were to be honest, inclusive, and globally relevant. We started co-creating lessons and we would teach them in our classrooms from across the country. We were fascinated with the conversations that were coming out of this work. It was our mission to include culture, history, economics, geography, civics, and sociology in the primary grades. Why? Because we felt that if our students learned at a young age to respect other cultures and how interconnected the world is, maybe children in the future wouldn't feel the need to behave in the ways that we'd been seeing in the media.

So . . . how did this end up in a book?
Well, the more we created, the more stories
we began to collect. Those stories would
sometimes end up on social media. At first,
we had a small group of teachers cheering
on this work. It was fresh, and at the time, not
a lot of primary teachers were focusing on
global content. The more time passed, the
more stories were shared until one day a friend
said to us, "You guys could totally write a book
about this." We scoffed. Us? A book? *Nah!*

We sat on the idea for a while. Eventually
we began to share these stories and
examples with educators at conferences
and professional development (PD) trainings
at various schools. The response from the
teachers whom we worked with was palpable.
It was the dreaded imposter syndrome
issue. Even though educators all over the
country were telling us that we'd inspired

them to teach differently, grow cultural intelligence, and cultivate globally connected learners . . . we had to convince ourselves that our story was actually worth sharing. That might be something that you need to hear. We hope that the recurring theme of this book is clear: if you are truly passionate about something—to the point where you feel like you might explode if you don't share this fascinating thing with the world—you don't need permission. Not these days. There are so many ways to share your expertise with the world, and writing a book is just one.

Now, in the following, we share what we've learned about publishing a book. In no way is this going to be an exhaustive list, but rather we will speak to the various modes that we've had experience with. We didn't know what we didn't know. Living and learning is good until you lose your hard-earned money, so we hope this will at least get you on the right track to research more about what might work best for you.

EBOOK PUBLISHING

We want to tell you about the easiest publishing we've ever done: ebook publishing! These books are relatively quick, easy, and cheap to produce on your own, and can be uploaded to any platform that allows digital items to be sold. An ebook is an electronic book—basically an online document that looks "book-like." You put your ideas together and then share them with others via an electronic device like a phone, tablet, or computer. When we began creating social studies lessons for our students, we (unknowingly) got into the business of publishing ebooks.

We would research a topic and then synthesize the information in a way our students could better understand it. We found some sites that allowed us to use their free, stock photos, and we put it all together in a book format using PowerPoint. Once we began sharing these books on social media, we quickly learned that other teachers wanted access to these books as well. They either didn't have the time to put them together on their own or just had no desire to, but they didn't mind paying a few dollars for it to be done for them. At the time of this writing, we have published (and sell) over 100 ebooks covering various educational topics for students and educators! (See Figures 6.1 and 6.2.)

The Pros of Ebook Publishing

The sky's the limit. Write your words, grab some clip art or photos to support it, and you're done. It really is that simple if you have an idea and time.

Figure 6.1 Resource eBook Covers.

Figure 6.2 Resource eBook Covers.

The Cons of Ebook Publishing

Your platforms may be limited because you likely won't be getting an International Standard Book Number (ISBN) (more on that later) or technically publishing it. You're really just publishing an online document that resembles a book.

SELF-PUBLISHING

You have an idea for a book. Great! There are ways to get your book published without involving anyone else because self-publishing is all you from start to finish. These days, you can upload your book to a hosting service like Amazon Kindle Direct Publishing (KDP) or IngramSpark and be on your way. LaNesha shares her experiences with self-publishing.

LaNesha's Self-Publishing Journey

I ended up publishing two books completely on my own. They were picture books intended for children (Figure 6.3). (Please note, we have an entire section about illustrators at the end of this chapter.) I had a very clear vision for this book, so I began by opening up a PowerPoint file and typing the words that I wanted

Figure 6.3 Pages from the book, Alpert.

on each page. I wanted to illustrate it myself, but had no clue how to go about it. I ended up drawing my illustrations with a pack of Crayola crayons and a black marker. I drew each piece individually (like a tree, a table, etc.), and with my phone, I snapped a photo of each image and loaded the image on my computer. There are tons of websites that allow you to upload an image and they will remove the background! Once the background was removed, those pictures that I drew basically became like clip art. I could drag and drop the images wherever I wanted to on the page. I could resize them and copy/paste where I needed to.

Once I had the book formatted in my PowerPoint file, I saved the entire thing as a Portable Document Format (PDF) file. From there, I had to decide if I wanted to upload it to Amazon KDP or IngramSpark, but the thing to think about there is the pricing. You'll likely not make a good amount of money on those platforms unless your book truly takes off (which it could!). If you do that, you have to purchase an ISBN. The ISBN is a unique identifier for a book that tells its format and other important information. If you're going to sell the book, you need to secure an ISBN. I didn't find that terribly difficult. There are websites, articles, and YouTube videos that walk you exactly through the process if you search "how to get an ISBN number for my book."

I initially decided against publishing my book on one of the self-hosted websites and opted to have mine printed locally. I Googled "local printers near me" and found a company that had decent rates and printed a gorgeous book for me. I literally called the company and said, "If I have a PDF file, can you turn it into a book?" The response was, "Absolutely." The company sent me one copy and it was lovely. From there, I'd place small orders until I had earned enough cash to buy bigger orders because I didn't want to go into too much debt with this venture.

We learned how to offer the book for sale on my website, which also meant that we had to learn how to ship the books from our home. It was daunting at first, but literally, YouTube taught us. There are so many people who are running businesses from home that it didn't take long to figure out. It also didn't take long for us to realize that this was not for us.

At first, it was super-exciting to see orders coming in. We loved to print the labels, bring in the boxes of books from the garage, put on some music and have a packing party! Look at us! Packing and shipping like some bosses, *whoo-hoo!* After the 40th packing party, though? Over it. Not for us. It was exhausting. With that comes a new job: customer service. The emails that read "My book says it was delivered, but I don't have it!" and "I ordered this yesterday, why isn't it here?" You have to respectfully explain that you're not in control of the packages after they leave and that you are also not Amazon Prime two-day shipping, and that all got old.

We ended up on a freelance marketplace website (where people offer their skill sets) and we hired someone to take my book files and upload them to a self-publishing site for us. We could have figured it out, but opted to hire out for that job. Now, the book is available for sale without us having to pack and ship (and now I'm ready to actually party)!

I wrote another book that consisted purely of fonts and icons. I created the entire book using PowerPoint and clip art that I paid for from a website that offers icons for commercial use (Figure 6.4). This book took the same journey as the book that I illustrated. We spent time selling and shipping, and eventually, that book ended up being uploaded to a self-publishing platform.

I published these books on my own because I had a crystal-clear vision for what I wanted them to look like. I also felt that I was capable of achieving the look I was going for without hiring an illustrator or graphic designer. However, there is *nothing* wrong with hiring out. If you have creative ideas but just need someone to make it visually appealing, there are people who do just that. I will say that I think it's incredibly empowering to

Figure 6.4 This book was created entirely in Power-Point with fonts and icons that were purchased for commercial use.

learn your craft and have the ability to do it yourself. That took a lot of time and practice learning how to do everything there is to do in PowerPoint, but now I feel as though I can create just about anything I want! I can choose to outsource, but if I don't, I've got the skill set because I put in the time to learn how to use these programs. Now, on the other hand, I do have another picture book in the works where the illustration needs were beyond my scope of ability, so I hired an illustrator. We will get into that journey later, but hopefully, you can see that publishing your own book is more than possible. If you don't mind doing the shipping yourself, then you won't have any barriers. Even if you don't want to deal with shipping, you can still find a way to handle your distribution needs; it may just take a few more steps. There are definitely multiple ways to get your book published on your own. My favorite thing about publishing on my own is that I can move on my own timeline! I don't have to wait on anyone or be rushed through a certain step because someone else is waiting. I can move as quickly or slowly as I'd like.

The Pros of Self-Publishing

You get to make the rules. It's all you. Every single decision is up to you. No one will tell you "no"! Lots of authors who publish in more traditional ways will complain about having creative differences and the publishing company might win on those. You can choose to market however you want.

The Cons of Self-Publishing

You get to make the rules. It's all you. Every single decision is up to you. No one will be there to point out the typos or formatting mistakes if there are any. You may need to pay someone to proofread and give you feedback on the content. There may be inconsistencies that you don't notice. You're on your own for marketing. You'll have to figure out how to get your book in front of people. There are tons of groups and organizations where independent publishers come together and find ways to support one another. In a group like that you might find out about a specific bookstore that supports indie (independent) authors or book fairs that you may be able to sell your copies to.

HYBRID PUBLISHING

So, what is *hybrid publishing*? Well, essentially, you pay; you're published! More specifically, you would pay a one-time fee up front for a list of services to be rendered in publishing your book. Some of these companies will charge you up front, but then they will take little to no royalties on sales. The author is typically in the driver's seat with these kinds of companies. I (LaNesha) had an experience with a company like this before I realized exactly what it was.

I had a friend who was a published author who reached out to me and encouraged me to write a book. I already had an idea for a new book that needed an actual publisher (not me and my Crayolas) and I thought that this was perfect. This friend connected me with his publisher and explained that if I paid money up front, the publisher would publish my book, make it available for purchase everywhere, and *wouldn't take any royalties*! I seriously thought that was too good to be true. Well, in some ways it was. I would learn quite a few lessons through this experience.

One lesson was the fact that I didn't realize that I would basically be on my own for this book. I envisioned working with a team of people who were going to give me solid feedback on the wordiness of my book or catch inconsistencies in the illustrations. My contract stated in very simple terms that a round of "developmental edits" would be made, but I didn't really know what that meant. While some edits and revisions were made to my book, it was far from being ready to be published, in my opinion. I had a friend who owned her own publishing company graciously take a look at my book after I'd shared what was happening with my publisher. In one hour, this friend affirmed that it was far too long, inconsistent in some areas, and she pointed out mistakes in my illustrations that I'd totally missed! For example, she told me that at one point in the book I referred to a certain day of the week, but later in the book, a calendar illustration alluded that it was a different day! She also noted that my main character was a different size on multiple pages and that the proportions were off. These were the kinds of things that I *thought* my publisher would catch but didn't. I can also recall the time when my book was sent to me for the first time. The illustrations that I was in love with looked as though they were produced on a 2003 laser printer. I couldn't believe it. It wasn't until I held the book that I realized that there would be no shiny, glossy illustrations like I'd seen from my friend who connected me to this company. I found out that he actually had the file sent overseas and the book was printed and shipped to the United States for him to sell. *Whaaaat?* I didn't know how to do all that! Turns out, my book was to be going to be uploaded to a huge website where books can be printed on demand based on sales. That meant that the quality of the book wasn't necessarily going to look like the books you see on the shelves of Barnes & Noble.

Not only that, but when I finally held a printed copy, there was a typo on the *spine* of my book! A typo. On the spine. *Of my book*! The book I was so proud of. I told my publisher and they sort of laughed and said, "Oh, yeah, things like that happen. You may want to ask a few friends to read it and check for typos. Then we'll just fix it and re-upload the file!" All I could think was, "*Excuse me?*" Oh, there was a lot to learn.

I would ask about correcting certain things, and I was basically told that it was "fine" and no one would notice this and that. I was so sad! I read hundreds of picture books and I know full-well how parents, teachers, and students pay close attention to all of the details in a picture book. Our academic standards even require it!

I also started to get the feeling that this publisher really wanted to just get this book to the finish line because I had already paid my money, so now it seemed like it was just something on their list that needed to be checked off. This was not the journey that I had signed up for! I grew increasingly frustrated because I was out quite a bit of money and I found myself staying up late at night making edits and revisions that I felt like they should've done.

What I couldn't work out and what I want to make sure to address is the fact that I couldn't work out how they were making money at a company like this. In my head, I was thinking, "If these publishers are only taking some money up front, but never making anything on the royalties . . . how do they make their money?" Well, it all started to make sense once I found out that publishing companies like this can publish *lots* of authors. It all changes when you realize that they can crank out 20 to 30 authors' books in one month! *Now* I see exactly where their money is coming from. So, what I've learned is that companies like these have figured out how to take a book, get it printed, and posted on a website that will allow for it to be printed and sold anywhere—and if you're willing to pay upfront, they'll make that happen for you—which is fine; I just didn't realize that that was what I was signing up for.

So, what happened? After a meeting where I laid out all of my concerns, I was basically told that it was my book and that they weren't responsible for how happy I was with my work. *Ouch.* I ended up parting ways with this company and getting a portion of my money back. I chalked it up to a "you-live-and-learn" situation that I have shared with lots of people who ask me how I published my books. I think if I had gone into this publishing situation with the awareness that I have now, I could've been much more mindful. I wouldn't have expected for them to give me the level of editing and revision that I was looking for. It probably would have been a much less frustrating experience if I'd known, but I didn't! That's why I am making sure to include this information in this book. If you're ever in a position to publish your book with a hybrid publisher, ask lots of questions before you sign a contract.

As for my book, I ended up getting picked up by the friend/publisher that found all of the inconsistencies in my book. You're probably thinking, "If you had this friend all along, why didn't you just work with her to begin with?" Well, for one thing, we weren't "friends" really, but rather online chatting buddies. I didn't really know her like that. Also, she actually did offer to do my book but she'd told me that she only took on what she could handle, and that my book wouldn't be able to happen until the following year. My impatient self decided to pass and go with the hybrid publisher. What do they say about hindsight? So, yes, she graciously decided to take my book on and as I write this book, it is currently being broken down and built back up—and I'm *so* glad about it. It was a long journey, but I'm glad it's being done right.

I will say that this kind of publishing company—hybrid style—is probably ideal for the author who wants to write a book that is more in their control and just wants help with the distribution. As a matter of fact, had I known about this kind of publishing option, I might have pitched my self-published books that I mentioned before to a company like this. So, I personally am not "knocking" hybrid publishing, I'm just hoping that you learn from my experience and educate yourself before jumping in!

The Pros of Hybrid Publishing

They'll offer light suggestions, but you are really in the driver's seat. It'll be available everywhere to purchase online.

The Cons of Hybrid Publishing

You need to have a tight manuscript that you feel good about. If you're doing a picture book, you may not get the crisp illustrations you are looking for if it is going to be uploaded to a "print on demand" server.

EDUCATIONAL PUBLISHING

There are lots of publishing companies that specialize in certain types of publishing, and there are plenty of publishers that focus on educational topics. These are the companies that you will usually find in the back of your school PD books, and in some cases, textbook companies may have smaller imprints that publish books for educators. Educational publishing companies are always looking for a fresh voice or fresh content to inspire and support teachers. If you have an idea, don't think that it can't be fleshed out in a book. *It can.* We didn't believe we had enough to say about our topic, either. We worked with an editor at our educational publishing company (shout-out to Dave Burgess Consulting, Inc.) for our book *Unpack Your Impact*, and we ended up having more than enough to say. It's so hard for some people to believe that they could be an author because the job seems to be reserved for serious academics who reach a certain elite level. We've found that if you have a message, a framework, and a set of ideas that can be shared, you can be an author. Write down what you do. Spare no details. If you work with an educational publishing company, it will have editors of all kinds to help you figure out how granular you need to be or where to add more details.

How do you break into these publishing companies? From our experience, you submit a book proposal. You will likely be asked to include a cover letter that will allow you to introduce yourself, give your reasoning for writing this book, and reasons why you think that particular publishing company would be a good fit for your book. You may be asked to include your resume and other pertinent information that would speak to the credibility of the book you are planning to write. You'll want to think through some of these questions as the publisher will likely want to know:

- Who is the intended audience?
- How will you organize this book?
- Why is this topic needed?
- Is this content evergreen, meaning is it applicable all year (vs. holiday content, e.g.)?
- How do you plan to get examples of student work, photos, and so on?
- What books would you consider as competition for this book?

From there, the publisher will likely want to see a sample chapter and a working table of contents so that it can get a feel for the direction that you are wanting to take. We said it before and we'll say it again: shoot your shot. Why not? You never know if the content that you are hoarding in your brain could be exactly what another educator is looking for. Your gift could make all the difference for a brand-new educator looking to find their bearings or the 30-year veteran looking to try something new.

We get into the idea of social media more in Chapter 1, so for now, we will just put this out there: awareness only helps. If you have an online presence, then that makes it easier for people to see exactly what you have to offer and the proof is literally posted. We live in a time where one of the first things we do when we meet someone new is to Google them. What is going to come up if someone Googles you? Anything? The formula for us was that we believed in our work and wanted to share it. We didn't care if we shared it with only 30 people as long as we could share it. Once we shared it, then we had primed ourselves for any opportunities that might come our way. Remember, you never know when the "right" set of eyes will fall on your work. Be ready!

Naomi's Journey in Educational Publishing

I had a bit of a different journey to get my first picture book published. I knew that I wanted to share a story with educators and caregivers to help them navigate conversations about skin color, but I wasn't sure where to start. After receiving some inspiration from LaNesha, I decided to self-publish. I looked up guidelines for writing children's books and I got to work. I wrote, edited, and revised a manuscript to tell my story. I titled it *Micah's Big Question*. I reached out to a few people I knew who published picture books and asked for their advice. A friend of mine, Tara Martin, talked to me about pagination. This was a fancy, new word for me to add to my vocabulary that just meant I needed to break my manuscript up into chunks, the way they might be placed on a page in a real book.

After I finished that process, I began to think about the illustrations I wanted that would bring my words and characters to life. I knew that I wanted my illustrator to be a Black artist, so I turned to Instagram and started sifting through a few hashtags. I looked through #artist, #illustrator, #illustrations and other keywords of that nature. When I found posts featuring illustrations that I liked, I tapped on them and tried to find out as much as I could about the illustrator. There were a few illustrators I found that were already signed with agencies, meaning, you couldn't just hire them off the street. You would have to go through their agents; they only worked with well-established children's book companies, and they were too expensive for what I could afford to pay out of pocket anyway. I kept searching and I finally found what I was looking for. I happened upon the page of a young, Black, college-aged woman whose Instagram feed was filled with the style of illustrations I was seeking for my book. I sent her a direct message (DM) and explained that I was trying to self-publish, needed an illustrator, and was obsessed with her sketches. She agreed to become my illustrator and that was the beginning of our partnership. After sending her my manuscript, I paid her for some initial sketches to see if she truly matched the vibe I was looking for with my book. The sketches were incredible, and we agreed to move forward together.

Now, here's where my journey takes a turn from self-publishing to educational publishing. Some background knowledge to keep in mind about me is that while all of this picture-book writing was going on, I was simultaneously still creating resources and marketing them, designing merch for my online store, working on virtual speaking engagements, being a mom of two, a wife, and a whole human. It was a lot, and the thought of getting the book to the finish line on my own began to overwhelm me. I decided to reach out to Dave and Shelley Burgess, who had published our first book *Unpack Your Impact*. I didn't reach out to them initially because they don't usually publish children's books, but at the point I was at, I figured there was no harm in asking. I am so glad I did because after I pitched the book and showed them the illustrations, they were on board with helping me get my book published through their company. They reviewed my manuscript and sent it to the right people on their team so it could go through developmental editing of ideas and another few rounds of editing for grammar and punctuation. They worked with my illustrator, and I provided ongoing feedback for *Micah's Big Question*. I am so grateful and thankful for them believing in my book and making the publishing process so enjoyable.

Did I mention I wrote 20 more children's books and I did it all in less than a year? Cue the freeze-frame of me and the audio saying, "You're probably wondering how I ended up here." So as we mention in Chapter 1, the powerful role of social media in your business life cannot be stressed enough. It can help us build relationships and make connections from all over the world. During the height of the pandemic, like many others, my 4-year-old son was home from school for the foreseeable future, and I was homeschooling him. I was also juggling having a 5-month-old at home, so I didn't have all the time in the world to plan and implement one-on-one lessons each day. Enter Khan Academy Kids. I discovered this educational app and began using it daily with my son. It was a teacher's dream come true. The lessons were engaging and interactive, and my son looked forward to Khan Academy time each day. I wanted to share this find with other caregivers and parents who may have been looking for a way to support their children at home, so I began posting about Khan Academy Kids on my social media account. I would share what my oldest son was working on and tag the account in my stories. The company would always thank me for sharing and that was that. But a few months later, Caroline Hu, the Vice President of Khan Academy Kids, reached out to me personally and wanted to set up a Zoom to discuss a potential partnership. My oldest son and I were invited to be guests on the company's YouTube show *Circle Time with Khan Academy Kids*, and we got to talk about the social justice topics that they noticed I had been sharing about on my own Instagram account and that they were passionate about as well.

A few months later, people at the company reached out again. They were looking to expand the digital library in their app and they wanted to know if I would be interested in authoring 20 books for them. I said "yes," and began the process of writing for Khan Academy Kids. We started by brainstorming a list of ideas, and they let me know which ideas would be great fits for their library. I was able to write my stories and give ideas for what the art on each page should look like. Via Google Drive, we were able to work as a team, sharing ideas, edits, and questions to finalize each book. There were many parameters to keep in mind: vocabulary, Lexile level, and story lesson had to be carefully considered because of the age group these stories are geared toward. Each book was about 10–11 pages and included comprehension questions for children to ponder. The company used its own illustrators to create the art, but I was able to give feedback and I really appreciated that. I was even able to use my own voice to record 10 of the books that are now available on its app! I am grateful for their guidance and insight for each book every step of the way.

The Pros of Educational Publishing

You will get lots of support with your writing. Editing, formatting, all the things that need to happen to get the book on the shelf will be handled for you. You may or may not receive an advance on your book; it depends on your contract and the company that you go with. The publisher will also help with marketing because shared success is important to all.

The Cons of Educational Publishing

You may have to work on a tight schedule or have a creative difference of opinion. This is a good thing to ask before you sign a contract because you want to publish a book that you can be proud of. Ask the publisher who gets the "final say" if there is a difference of opinion.

TRADITIONAL BOOK PUBLISHING

When we say "traditional book publishers," we are talking about the publishing houses that you would probably be able to name off the top of your head if you were asked to. Before this book, neither one of us had an actual experience with a traditional book company—although we would be lying if we said we didn't dream of it. The company that we are writing this book for actually reached out to us (shout-out to Jossey-Bass). As we understand it, that's not normal. That is a result of the "right eyes" landing on our work and social media presence. But, we (and now you) know that it is possible!

We do have several friends who have published with traditional companies and we have learned some insightful information from them. Publishing with a major house is obviously much more difficult to do. Most of the people whom we know (who have books that show up on the *New York Times* best-seller list) have full-blown agents, marketing teams, and all those kinds of "fancy" things. When we would talk to them about their journey, we were advised to get ourselves a book agent if we really wanted to get "serious." We tried that, and it didn't work out too well, but we may consider that in the future. Honestly, we don't know enough about it and we would have to do some research. See? Research. I said that on purpose because I wanted to quickly illustrate for you that any and everything we'd set out to do over the past 10 years had to start with some form of research. That hasn't changed!

We've also heard stories that make us not so sure that that is the route that we would *ever* want to take. We've heard stories from our friends that would make us terrified to lose that much control over our work. Apparently, with traditional publishing companies can come huge differences of opinion from illustration styles and word choices all the way down to whether or not names of authors/illustrators with names that might suggest a particular ethnicity would be bad for marketing. Wow! Some authors have shared that they didn't even get to pick their own illustrator for their book. Those are the sorts of things that would probably make us scream. So, for us, at this point in time, it seems like it would be really cool to consider, but we would have lots of questions that we would need to get figured out before we ever considered publishing with a company that would hold way more power.

The Pros of Traditional Book Publishing

You're likely to make much more money! You'd have an agent making things happen for you, which will increase the marketing that is available to you.

The Cons of Traditional Book Publishing

The timelines are out of your control. You could lose some of the creative control; we recommend making peace with that if you go this route!

So, we've shared quite a bit of our journey. We tell you this because hearing someone else's journey can show you what might be possible for you. It's important to note that we personally know some educators who have published books in one or more of the ways we've listed in this chapter. That was inspiring to us! Teachers, just like us, writing books? If they could do it, why couldn't we? It took us some time (we're talking *years*) to decide that we were going to go for it and we are so glad we did. What stories do you have inside of you that can inspire another educator or child?

A Note about Illustrators

If you have a picture-book idea that has been brewing in your mind, you're probably thinking about the process of securing an illustrator. This would mostly apply to the publishing that you would do on your own or through a hybrid publisher, but we will share what we've learned.

We imagine that back in the day finding an illustrator would have been nearly impossible unless you had one in your inner circle. But remember, we are here *now* with the internet at our fingertips. Just about anything is possible!

Once we knew the picture-books we wanted to put out into the world, we began to imagine what the illustrations might look like. Then we went to social media and began looking through hashtags. We didn't even know what we were looking for, so we just tried to find some information about what it would even take to hire an illustrator. We searched keywords like #illustrator, #diverseauthors, #childrensbookillustrators, and #artist and began to look through the pages of independent and represented artists that showcased the styles we felt would best fit with our stories.

We sent them messages explaining our visions and that we were looking to partner with amazing illustrators who brought our visions to life. Now, don't get us wrong. It wasn't all sunshine and rainbows. We talked to some artists who were already very established and only worked with publishing companies, and some who were too expensive for our book budget. We also realized that many amazing illustrators could only be worked with through their agency, and that meant that you were going to need to be able to pay for that time. But we kept on searching until we found the perfect matches for us—and we did! We ended up finding artists who weren't currently working for an agency. We sifted through their online portfolio (aka Instagram feed) and asked what their process was to illustrate a book. Some of the illustrators we used had illustrated some books before but others were artists who hadn't even considered illustrating a book for children. Publishing these books on our own (or hybrid) meant that we were looking to hire out for art. Because we are paying for their art, it was a one-time fee to compensate them for the skills and time. This is definitely an investment, but it may not have had to be. I'm willing to bet that if we'd talked to our illustrators, they might have been open to a partnership with shared royalties. We made our own rules for this long, so why not? Can't hurt to try to work something like that out.

TIPS FOR GETTING STARTED

Honestly? Open up a Microsoft Word document and start writing. Our books often began with an idea and then we went straight to the laptop to try to get it down. We are extremely visual, so as we had an idea for what we wanted the book to look like, we'd start crafting it on our computers. This is important because you need to make sure that this book idea is a thing. If you can create an entire manuscript that reads well and feels good, you can begin the journey toward finding a publishing option that works for you.

Chapter 7

Public Speaking

We open this chapter by saying: if the thought of public speaking terrifies you, you are in good company! We can assure you with all certainty that never in a million years did we see ourselves becoming public speakers in our profession. We can both remember years ago being asked to stand up in front of a staff meeting and share what we had learned at a training that we'd attended. It was the most uncomfortable thing! It was not something we really enjoyed, but would do because we promised we would if we were allowed to go to that training. With trembling voices and sweaty palms, we would stand up, say what we needed to say, and scurry back to our seats, where our grade-level teams would be waiting for us with reassuring looks on their faces. How terrifying! So you can imagine what those versions of ourselves must think of the work that we do today! We will get into those specifics later, but for now, just know that even if you feel as though you could never be a public speaker, don't write it off yet! You never know! You could be really great at it. As usual, we will share our journey and hopefully you will see that literally anything is possible if it's something you want to explore.

We'll start by qualifying some terms that we will use in this chapter. What do we mean when we say *speaking*? We mean hosting professional development (PD) sessions, submitting sessions to be considered for conferences, or providing keynote speeches. Honestly, we mean those things and everything in between. There are countless opportunities for educators to speak. We've learned that school districts, educational organizations, and event planners are constantly on the hunt for fresh messages from impactful speakers. And remember, your social media presence can act as a resume that allows others to see that you know your stuff and you know it well. We cover some of the main speaking opportunities lower down; first, we want to share our experiences. Before you jump in, you should know that we have very different experiences with speaking. One of our journeys is a bit longer than the other, so you'll likely be able to identify with one story or the other.

OUR JOURNEYS WITH PUBLIC SPEAKING

Naomi's Journey

When I tell you that becoming a speaker was not something I would ever think I'd be getting paid to do, please believe. I am picturing myself trying out for the cheerleading squad in fifth grade and freezing in front of the judges because the entire auditorium was watching me. I was escorted away in tears by the team mascot. Fast forward two years later and I was in seventh grade awaiting my turn to give a speech in front of my language arts class. I was so nervous, but I got up and started doing what I'd practiced a hundred times the night before. It was going well until I heard one of my classmates laugh and say, "I can't even hear her." That was it. Game over. Cue the lump in my throat and the tears down my cheeks. I cried on my index cards and could no longer read them. It was a mess, and so was I. And now let's jump to eleventh grade. I was smarter and already knew speaking in front an audience wasn't for me. A few solo speeches were due in some of my classes, but I did a few calculations and realized I could take a zero on all of my class speeches and still get a B+ or an A–. I skipped them all. I was the kid that took the zero.

When I became a teacher, I already knew leading PD sessions and conferences just wasn't for me, and I was more than okay with that. I just stayed in my lane. It was a comfortable lane. I liked my lane.

Little did I know my lane had a fork in the road. As I began to share my ideas and expertise on social media, conferences and schools began reaching out to me for speaking engagements. They wanted to pay me to talk in front of other adults. This wasn't my lane, but the money I was making in the classroom wasn't always enough, so the thought of taking on an education-related job was appealing. I accepted a few conference gigs, but ultimately decided it wasn't for me.

What I didn't realize is that it's not that speaking wasn't for me, it was that speaking about things I wasn't passionate about wasn't for me. In school and as an adult at work I was always told what to speak about. When I finally began to find my niche in the teaching world and online, I realized that I had a lot to say and wanted to share it with as many people as possible. I began to see that through speaking and impacting others, I could have a bigger impact on children, which is my ultimate goal. When a popular education conference approached me and asked if I would share my passions with educators around the country, I was still nervous, of course, but I was also excited.

Guess what year I presented at my first conference, wasn't that nervous, and felt like I did an incredible job? 2022—the same year this book got published. At the time of this writing, I am gearing up for four more conferences and I can't wait to share my knowledge with others.

Whether you are in the classroom or not, making time for a heavy speaking schedule can be tricky. Planning flights, coordinating schedules, arranging childcare, and balancing work can be overwhelming. To try to stay ahead of this, I emailed my current principal the dates I would have to miss this school year, so I don't have to worry about timidly asking for time off and feeling guilty about calling out. I don't love taking time away from my students, but when it's time well spent pouring into other educators, I can see how a few absences from work are worth it.

LaNesha's Journey

Honestly, I'm not sure how I started to gain interest in the area of PD. I think it might have started when I attended a very impactful PD that really motivated me to go back into my classroom and shift some practices in my instruction. Once I started to see those shifts yield really amazing results, I started to develop and try out my own strategies and ideas more and more. When you are getting results in the classroom, people want to know what you're doing. Not only that, but when something that you truly believe in is working well, you start to feel as though you want to share it.

Now, I will say that while speaking really may not be for everyone, that doesn't mean that you should write it off. Why? Well, if you would have asked me five years ago if I would ever be a speaker, I would have said, "Oh, no way. . .speaking is definitely not for me." I would have missed out on so many amazing opportunities. Over the years, somehow I have found myself in the same rooms as celebrities, politicians, authors, and really amazing change-makers because I stepped into the world of public speaking. Do I say that to brag? I mean, a little bit! Shoot. . .I have been afforded some amazing opportunities that I'm incredibly grateful for. No, I'm kidding. I really don't say that to brag. I say that because I am still in disbelief. One of my favorite things to do is picture myself in my classroom just a few short years ago enjoying my time as a teacher, but getting this itch to have a larger impact. I didn't really know how to manifest those feelings into action. We mention this a few times in this book, but you may not feel that "itch" because you don't believe in yourself. I know how corny that sounds, but it's true! When I was asked to lead my first PD that awful imposter syndrome jerk showed up strong. As I sat to make my presentation I kept thinking about how all of the teachers would roll their eyes and not want to listen to me. I created handouts and pictured them barely looking at it or tucking it away in a folder never to be consulted again. I thought I wasn't established enough or that they would question my credibility because I wasn't a famous author or researcher. I can tell you from first-hand experience that there will be people who may feel that way about you, but that's their business to take up with the person who believed in you enough to book you. You're capable of sharing greatness based on your experience, expertise, and proven success.

I delivered my first PD for a school that was trying to improve its reading instruction. I had been successful with the strategies that I was using at the time, and the school asked me to come share. Y'all? I was so nervous. I decided to adopt the old adage "Fake it till you make it" and walked in that room with the confidence of a tenured college professor. I just decided to go for it and I was thrilled when I started to see heads nod as I was speaking. They started to ask questions! I had them do some group activities to process what we were talking about, and they didn't stuff my handouts away! They actually used them. I was thrilled when I got an email a few days later from the principal thanking me for sharing my strategies and letting me know that a check was in the mail for me. What? Me, a whole speaker? (Looks in the mirror whispering, "You go, girl.")

I had no idea what to charge for this, and looking back on it, I basically did this training for free. But the fact that it got me over the hump of my first experience was definitely priceless. Over the next few years, I continued to do extremely small training sessions here and there, some for my school and some at the district level. I would have friends (teachers, instructional coaches, and admins) who worked at other schools ask if I would come and speak for them. It was so exciting!

What I've finally realized about speaking is the moment you have something that you are extremely comfortable talking about (because you know it so intimately), speaking becomes a lot less scary. I knew my content inside and out, so for me to walk somebody else through my process was no big deal. That's when it dawned on me that all of the times that I have been asked to share in front of my peers before typically involved me sharing what I learned at another training. It was someone else's content. I had an understanding of it, but it wasn't *my* content. That meant that I didn't know everything there was to know about that topic, so it made me extremely nervous to talk about it. But when it's yours—*your* lesson, *your* strategy, *your* story—telling it is much more comfortable.

The more I began to share my passion for social studies education on social media, the more opportunities I found for speaking. One year I was approached by a huge conference that was created by a group of educators. Conference representatives asked me if I would like to come and do a session on social studies. They told me they had been watching my work and they were impressed by my ideas and thought more teachers should hear about it. I was befuddled. Honestly, I was just like, "I'm over here, minding my business, sharing my passions, and now they want me to come to this conference and present a session? Wow." I couldn't believe it. It was one of those things where I was completely terrified, but I knew I was going to do it because I didn't want to miss that opportunity. Joining this conference ended up being a great opportunity for me. It was the first "big break" for me because I was able to speak to so many educators at one time. Before this conference, I was only speaking to small groups of educators in a school setting. This conference brought in people from all over the country. With every passing conference, I ended up talking to people who would come up to me after the session and ask if I did PD with other schools. I was so grateful that I could say, "Yes, I do!" I was glad that I had had some experience working with schools prior to this conference. I was asked to come and share the same message that I had presented at the conference in schools outside of my state. I couldn't believe it. One summer I found myself in Atlanta; Little Rock, Texas; and Florida being booked to do PD sessions at various schools and conferences. It truly was surreal.

What I will tell you about this speaking world is that pricing is extremely hard to figure out. I couldn't tell if I was charging way too little or way too much. I remember one year I was going to muster up the courage to charge $1,500 for my half-day training. I was going to fly there, get a hotel, get to the school, deliver the training, and then fly back home. The person hosting was gracious enough to say that that wasn't nearly enough to cover my travel plus my work. She could have paid me $1,500, but thankfully, she said that they had a budget of $4,200 that they could offer. That covered all of my travel and accommodations, and I got to take home the extra cash to compensate me for the time I spent planning, preparing, and actually administering the session. The more I got into the speaking world and became friends with other people who did this kind of work, I got a better handle on appropriate rates to charge.

Most schools have budgets that they not only can spend, but *have* to spend. You'll find that if a school feels like your content is valuable, it will choose to invest some of that money in people that it feels will really help the school. I have seen teachers work with schools on everything from mindfulness and meditation to support teacher mental health all the way to literacy work-station task cards. The more I paid attention to the kinds of sessions people were offering, the more I saw what was possible. I simply didn't realize how wide the spectrum of topics was for teachers who wanted to break into speaking. There are definitely some stipulations and protocols that have to be followed when schools spend their PD money, but it is way more flexible than I thought. I've also found that charter schools and private schools aren't bound by many of those rules and are often looking for educators to come and deliver PD or keynotes to their staff members.

Another thing to know is that the "world" of public speaking for educators can be very small. Once you start speaking, you'll find that it is extremely common to network and get picked up by other organizations that are looking for speakers. You will begin to run into the same people at various speaking engagements. During a conference or summit, there's typically a speaker holding room of sorts where lots of networking conversations naturally occur in between sessions. The more you talk to people, the more connections are formed. Those connections often and usually turn into an invitation to be a guest speaker on a podcast or a conference that that speaker is a part of. I've seen this happen time and time again. Networking will keep you booked and busy if that is what you desire.

When I first started speaking, I was still in the classroom. For about four years I juggled full-time teaching, speaking at conferences, and offering PD for schools. Honestly? It wasn't healthy. There was a lot of flying out and flying back in at midnight so I could be at school the next morning. I was working for what seemed like every second of the day. One year I even purchased a trampoline for my own two children because my schedule had been so jam-packed with traveling that that was my apology gift. After that summer, I promised myself that I would not book myself that much ever again because I was unwilling to miss those precious moments with family. While it did take a lot of time away from them, my hope is that one day they understand that their parents we're trying to pay off debt, leave an inheritance for them, and have the ability to say "yes" when they asked to be on the ridiculously expensive competitive dance team or travel soccer team. Those are some of the things that drive us to bring in extra income using the passions that we have.

I am now able to share my journey of making social studies important again with educators on a regular basis. I'm also able to take a teacher who absolutely hates to teach writing and turn them into a teacher who adores it. I created a framework that worked for me for years and the moment I started sharing it with other educators who found it wildly successful, I knew it needed to be shared widely. The feedback was too powerful. That's how you know you've got something. You start sharing and you pay attention to the feedback that you're getting. What are people saying about it? Is it truly helping someone? If it is, then don't be selfish with it! Start sharing it. When something is really impactful, it'll speak for itself. You just have to put it out there.

Speaking is now a regular part of my job. As I write this book, I typically have two or three speaking engagements a month. Since the pandemic, the virtual option for speaking engagements has made speaking much easier. In full disclosure, while I did do public speaking inside of the classroom, it has been much more manageable outside of the classroom. If you are still in the classroom and want to start speaking and offering PD, you totally can. I did it for years. I would just caution you to be careful with the amount of work you take on so that you can stay healthy.

So, now you are privy to our journeys into speaking. We are going to follow up with some tips and thoughts about getting started and various platforms that are available.

CONFERENCES

Conferences are literally everywhere. I say this because I didn't realize it and maybe you don't, either. They just weren't on my radar because I rarely heard about them. Early in my career, I vividly remember a flier ending up in my school mailbox one day. I opened it and looked at this huge list of presenters and I remember asking myself how these teachers were given this opportunity. I didn't think much else of it then, but the thought was there. There are so many educational conferences (both in-person and online) that it would blow your mind. If you don't believe me, hop online and enter the term "teacher conference near me" and watch the list populate.

Start researching these conferences. Note when they happen and who is presenting. Look for the contact information and find out what it would take to be a presenter for that conference. There are conferences that are put on by organizations that have been around for decades, but there are also conferences that are newer that are put on by teams of educators who just have a passion for helping teachers. You'll want to have a session proposal at the ready (more on that follows). It is important to research the conferences that you are interested in presenting for. Get a feel for who runs these conferences, the teachers they serve, and honestly, do a vibe check. Is it more of a serious conference with highly academic sessions filled with jargon and acronyms? Or is it a loud, intense, hands-on science conference, for example, where the conference goers are going to be ready to dig in with some hands-on activities that the presenter will lead them in? All conferences have a "vibe" and that's great! You just have to check to see if you are on the same wavelength as the conference that you'd like to work for.

Understand that all conferences are different when it comes to accommodations and compensation. We've presented for conferences that handle all of our travel, food, hotels, and so on, and paid us for the session. We've also been contacted to present for conferences that ask you to pay your own way to them and present for free. It really depends on the organization, but it is something you definitely want to ask about before you agree. We have been able to get glimpses to the back end of conference planning and we immediately realized why some conferences charge so much money. Venues charge outrageous fees for little things! If a conference wants to remain successful, a budget is necessary. Lots of times this is directly tied to what you may be offered as a presenter. Starting with a smaller, maybe local, conference is a great way to get your feet wet. Keep your eyes open; there's probably a conference near you that you didn't even know about.

The Pros of Speaking at Conferences

Conferences provide great exposure. You'll be in rooms full of educators, admins, and instructional coaches. You never know who is in the room listening to what you have to say and what that could lead to. We've received emails from schools all over the country asking if we could come and deliver a similar PD session because of what they heard at our session at a conference. Conferences are a great way to network with educational professionals. Everyone is already primed to learn, chat, and connect. They make the perfect breeding ground to spark opportunities for future speaking engagements!

The Cons of Speaking at Conferences

The cons can include a busy travel schedule if you decide to try to speak at multiple conferences. If you're doing conferences while teaching full time (which LaNesha did for four years), then it can be tricky to request the days off, leave the sub teaching plans, and have enough energy. Another con is a varied pay scale. It's not easy to predict what you will be paid because conferences have their own budgets that they have to follow. If you are looking for a more steady cash flow, conferences may not provide that.

SCHOOL PD SESSIONS

Some schools will choose to use their funds to meet a specific need. The teachers and literacy coaches will often recommend someone to come to their school to host a session to meet that need. This is where you could come in! You can put together sessions that last an hour, three hours, half-day, or full day that will help to move a school in your area of expertise. We've seen schools bring in speakers to lead them in mindfulness exercises to get through the school day from teachers who were also passionate about self-care in the area of mindfulness. This isn't technically a session that will drive content, but if it improves the morale of the educators in the building, then that's a good investment for that school. The more people are able to know about you and your work, the more likely it is that you would be hired to do this kind of work. If it goes really well, we've found that school administrators have lots of other school administrator friends. We've often been approached by principals who got our information from a principal that we'd worked with, asking us to share the same content that we did at their friend's school. Does this seem overwhelming or unrealistic? Please understand that we knew none of this when we started. We've picked up trends along the way, and wanted to share them with you. I don't think I would have believed that these things happened in this way unless I experienced it for myself, but really, things like this happen all the time!

The Pros of Speaking at School PD Sessions

Working with specific schools or districts can really be a great opportunity to help educators implement your content or strategies. This is a great opportunity for you to get some facetime with educators and come alongside them as thought partners as they look to incorporate strategies and skills that you've brought. You can build tighter relationships with educators, and that will often result in more teacher buy-in, which will have the greatest impact on students.

The Cons of Speaking at School PD Sessions

Like speaking at conferences, working with schools and/or districts can result in lots of travel. It can also be a bit stressful because you might arrive at a school that really needs help, and while you will probably know how to help them solve all the world's problems, you're often only there for a few hours. It can be tricky to stay focused at times.

MAKING YOUR OWN PLATFORM

Another cool thing about this age we are living in? If you don't see what you are looking for, you can do what? Make it yourself. We have seen groups of educators come together to create their own conference, not only in-person but online as well. Virtual conferences exploded after the pandemic. We decided to do this. The two of us joined forces with two other educators and put on our own conference. We, along with Vera Ahiyya and MoNique Waters, decided that among the four of us, we had some solid ideas to share in the areas of math, reading, writing, and community building for primary classrooms. We found a platform that you could use to set up your conference and have people register. We created a name (Now That's What I Call Teaching) and hired another teacher who was able to design well to help us create our logo and branding items. From there, we each did an hour-long session that was prerecorded and uploaded to the platform. We also did one session in a panel-style format for conference-goers. The conference launched, and while our sessions were playing, we would hang out in the comments section to answer questions that might be asked. At the end of the session, we offered tons of free resources that teachers could download and use immediately. With the money that we charged, we paid the people who helped us (and paid for the platform) and split the rest four ways. The cool thing was that since it was prerecorded, we were able to offer a replay a few months later. It was a really fun way to have our own conference and earn some extra money. People do this all the time. We've seen educators come together to create virtual conferences around the topics of classroom design, STEM, music, art, middle school math, and even conferences for other educators who are looking to break into the world of entrepreneurship. There are so many more examples, but the point here is that you can make it happen. You can partner up with a few teachers and put your own work out there for people to sign up and take. If you are thinking that you don't have a following and how would anyone find out about your conference. . .offer mini-trainings for free! You're bound to get some traffic for offering a high-quality PD session for free. Then, once your awareness grows, you may decide to charge for your virtual conference. We think the fact that you can take control and make something happen is pretty cool.

The Pros of Making Your Own Platform

The biggest benefit of creating your own PD experience is simply the fact that you are in full control. You can put a session or program together that includes every facet that you feel to be important!

The Cons of Making Your Own Platform

It can be difficult to spread the word about your work when it's coming from you as opposed to people who present content under a bigger umbrella company. It's not impossible to spread the word, but it can be tough.

FREE PD VIA ONLINE PLATFORMS

Honestly, if you pay attention, there are *tons* of educators speaking via online platforms. They are offering PD through Facebook groups, Instagram live sessions, and definitely on YouTube. You may be thinking, "Yeah, but those don't pay any money!" Well, that's not entirely true. Recording short-form video is one way (out of many) to show up online and monetize those platforms. For example, once you reach a certain amount of watch hours on YouTube, you can choose to monetize your channel. That means that every time someone watches your channel, you could earn money. We can't really scoff at this like many of us used to do when someone would say that they want to be "YouTube famous." That's 100% feasible. People have earned tons of money from ads or partnerships on YouTube. You can also monetize your free content in other ways, but the platforms are always shifting! Focus on putting out good content consistently (because consistency really is key) and you can make those views work for you.

The Pros of Free PD via Online Platforms

Accessibility has got to be one of the biggest pros for providing free content online. If you have access to a smartphone, tablet, and some Wi-Fi, you have the ability to share ideas with others. This is a great way to establish yourself as the authority on your topic.

The Cons of Free PD via Online Platforms

It can be difficult to shift through and find quality content. You have to really work hard to set yourself apart from the thousands of other videos.

TIPS FOR GETTING STARTED

What can you start doing *now?* At some point you have to ask yourself: "What am I waiting for?" If you are reading this chapter and you're thinking, "You know what? I think I actually could see myself speaking one day," then get ready *now.* What's your idea? What would it look like to share it with other educators? Do you need to snap photos of the idea so that people can see it in action? Do you have stories and examples at the ready so that your point is crystal clear? You can begin to sketch out those ideas now. Like, *now.* Grab your pen; let's go:

Planning Your Talk

Session idea:

Intended audience:

Structure/flow:

    Open with:

    Examples:

    Activities for teachers to process:

    Research to include/share:

    Major take aways:

What content can you deliver in one hour?

What content can you deliver in three hours?

What content can you deliver in half a day?

How could your content be stretched to a full day?

What resources would be needed?

Can you deliver this content virtually?

What will set this training apart from others?

What questions will other educators likely have?

Chapter 8
Passion Projects

We have shared about creating resources, speaking engagements, designing and selling merch, becoming an author, developing courses, and more. We wanted to close this book by highlighting educator friends of ours who have been wildly successful in their businesses using their personal passions and incorporating them into the world of education. We chose to do this because:

1. We are proud of our friends.
2. The more examples you see can show you what's possible.
3. This will demonstrate what we've said before: the sky is the limit.

These people have grown their businesses over the years, and it is incredibly inspiring to watch. Seeing other people win just means that you can also win. You've got to get your attitude in check and go for it. Don't get discouraged and think that you have nothing to share. Just wait. We're going to share just *some* of the people whom we truly admire below. We encourage you to check them out. Visit their websites and social media handles. Look at their journeys and then continue dreaming. Your creative idea can be next!

PASSION ALERT: ADORABLE ACCESSORIES

Carlanda Miller, The Magical Teacher

We have a friend named Carlanda Miller (@TheMagicalTeacher). She loves to be stylish and dress in bright colors. She started making her own earrings to match her style and began offering them to other educators (Figures 8.1 and 8.2). She features her earrings with her adorable outfits and costumes on her social media platforms and website. We want to purchase every pair. They've been a hit! She has found a way to make her passion for darling accessories relevant to educators through her photos and marketing. Brilliant! A message from Carlanda:

> *"I truly believe that everybody has something unique about them that makes them magical! My passion is to help other people unlock the magic that is inside of them. In the classroom, I feel fulfilled watching my students reach milestones and goals and I also feel fulfilled helping other teachers spread magic in their classroom. My love of arts and crafts and fashion led me to start making earrings. When people wear my earrings it helps bring a little extra magic out of them."*

https://www.carlandathemagicalteacher.com/

Figure 8.1 Carlanda Miller-the Magical Teacher.
Source: https://www .carlandathemagicalteacher .com/, last accessed July 25, 2022

Figure 8.2 Carlanda's earrings.
Source: https://www .carlandathemagicalteacher .com/, last accessed July 25, 2022

PASSION ALERT: TEACHER TEES
Latrice Galloway, CEO Trendy Teacher Tees

Years ago, our friend Latrice Galloway (@trendyteacherz), who owns preschool, found herself at a teacher conference. She saw an extremely long line of educators waiting to buy something, but she didn't know what. She finally realized that all those teachers were in line to purchase a T-shirt that was designed for teachers. Latrice got the idea that she could be doing the exact same thing with her own creative designs and possibly have a line like that too (Figures 8.3 and 8.4). She knew she had her own style and figured there were other educators like her that would love her style too, and she was right. Trendy Teacherz was born and is an extremely

Figure 8.4 Latarice's t-shirt design.
Source: https://www .trendyteacherz.com/, last accessed July 25, 2022

Figure 8.3 Latrice Galloway, CEO of Trendy Teacherz.
Source: https://www.trendyteacherz .com/, last accessed July 25, 2022

successful business. She sends her adorable tees to educators, and they post pictures of her T-shirts, which help her promote her business. Another educator, Johora Warren, is her VA.

A message from Latrice:

"I always wanted to do something to express my love for fashion. I love dressing up . . . I love being a "fashionista." Being in the classroom and in my school every single day I was always dressed down, but I still wanted to make it cute! I decided to start making T-shirts for my staff and then it just grew into this business. Now, teachers all over the world get to express their love for teaching and fashion with our "Trendy Teacher Tees!"

https://www.trendyteacherz.com/

PASSION ALERT: STICKERS

Tamara Moore (@ifpencilscouldtalk)

We have a handful of friends who design the most adorable stickers that you've ever seen. These stickers adorn water bottles, laptop covers, notebooks, planners, and more. These stickers are often more than just "cute." They typically share a powerful message that is near to the causes and communities that they care about. We are typing this book from laptops that are adorned with their stickers this very moment! Tamara Moore sells gorgeous stationery, pencils, and stickers (Figure 8.5). A message from Tamara:

"I am deeply passionate about making school a safe, inclusive place for queer kids and I consider myself a creative person. Being able to combine my advocacy and talents with a small business has helped me feel more confident in the space I deserve to take up as a Black Queer educator. Giving teachers and people all over the world (!!!) items that can help them be visible in their support for the LGBTQ+ community makes me feel like change is possible and is coming."

https://www.etsy.com/shop/ifpencilscouldtalk

Figure 8.5 Tamara Moore, owner If Pencils Could Talk.
Source: https://www.etsy.com/ in-en/shop/ifpencilscouldtalk, last accessed July 25, 2022

PASSION ALERT: SELF-CARE FOR EDUCATORS

Sarah Forst, Founder The Designer Teacher LLC

Our friend Sarah Forst (@thedesignerteacher) noticed a big problem in education and started a venture to help with that problem (Figures 8.6–8.8). Via social media, educators were beginning to share how burned-out they were feeling. Like many of us, Sarah felt as though she couldn't make the much-needed systemic changes happen on her own, but she could provide some comfort items for teachers who needed a small pick-me-up. She created a subscription box that would go out to educators monthly! These curated boxes were filled with amazing items from lots of small and teacher-owned businesses. According to her website, each box includes inspirational art, bath and body items, on-trend accessories, and tasty treats to make your teacher heart happy. How incredible is that? She works with vendors to stock the boxes full of items that will encourage educators to take care of themselves. She even wrote a book called *The Teacher's Guide to Self-Care: Build Resilience, Avoid Burnout, and Bring a Happier and Healthier You to the Classroom.*

Here is a message from Sarah:

"After I left the classroom, I knew I wanted to stay connected to education and support teachers and students. Teacher Care Crate allowed me to use my background in design to help teachers practice stronger self-care. While I was no longer reaching students directly, I was helping their teachers take care of their well-being and hopefully have more sustainable careers in education. It's been immensely gratifying to hear from teachers that they look forward to their Teacher Care Crate every month and that it truly reminds them to practice self-care."

https://www.teachercarecrate.com/

Figure 8.6 Sarah Forst, Founder of Teacher Care Crate. *Source:* https://www.teachercarecrate.com/, last accessed under July 25, 2022

Figure 8.7 Sarah's book. *Source:* https://www.teachercarecrate.com/, last accessed under July 25, 2022

Figure 8.8 Sarah's care crate. *Source:* https://www.teachercarecrate.com/, last accessed under July 25, 2022

PASSION ALERT: INTERIOR DESIGN

Brittany Wheaton, Interior Designer

We have a friend named Brittany Wheaton (@brittanyjeltema). She has an eye for interior design (Figure 8.9). We're talking give this woman an empty room and in a few hours she will transform it into the most beautiful space you've ever seen. She took her love for designing and decorating, and moved it into the classroom. She has gone viral for her classroom flips and has worked with teachers all over the country to flip their classrooms into a beautiful and practical learning space for students. She has even flipped teacher workspaces to give educators useful and inviting spaces to plan lessons, grab coffee, or just take a minute to relax during their busy days. Brittany turned her love for design and classroom flips into a classroom decor business. She offers a

Figure 8.9 Brittany Wheaton, Interior Designer.
Source: Brittany jeltema

variety of items that educators can use to enhance their environments if they would like to.

Here is a message from Brittany:

"I've always had a passion for learning and teaching. However, it wasn't until I was introduced to curriculum design that I felt completely fulfilled as an educator. After discovering my passion for creating resources for teachers, I went back to school to get my master's degree in marketing. It was during that time that my perspective shifted and I truly learned how to get my resources in the hands of thousands of teachers and students—still making a difference in a way that so many teachers do. This path has also given me the opportunity to give back to educators and students through classroom makeovers and inclusive classroom decor. I see my business not only as a way to support my family, but as a unique way to create necessary change in the world of education."

https//: https://thesuperheroteacher.com/

PASSION ALERT: MUSIC

Franklin Willis, Founder of F. Willis Music

Franklin Willis (@fwillismusic) is a music teacher who has found a way of combining new-school trends with an old-school technique to create fun music education resources for teachers and students! He's turned his passion for teaching music into a book called *Edward's Rhythm Sticks*, developed a merchandise line for music advocates and music lovers, and creates stick routines for teachers to implement in their music lessons (Figure 8.10). He also holds workshops for music teachers during which he shares his strategies. Incredible!

Here is a message from Franklin:

"I feel fulfilled because I know that my education experiences are valid and that they matter. I had no idea that my sharing a song or a

chant would be something that other educators wanted to help build engagement with their students in elementary music. And so now it's fun! When I have a song on my heart or on my mind, I can sing it, I can write it, and I can share it with other folks. I can also be compensated for what I create, which has been a blessing. It's a blessing to be in the educational field, doing what I love, but also being compensated for my talents and time. If you're a teacher or educator who knows how to teach an old concept in a new way, I encourage you to put that out into the universe. Put it out into the world; you never know the impact that you will have. So, you just have to take the jump . . . you have to take the leap and have faith in your gift and your abilities."

https://www.fwillismusic.com/

Figure 8.10 Franklin Willis, Founder fwillismusic.
Source: https://www .fwillismusic.com/, last accessed under July 25, 2022

PASSION ALERT: FASHION

April Graves, Teacher Style Influencer

April Graves (@aprilalldae) has a passion, and it is fashion (Figure 8.11). She uses her social media channels to share her daily looks, but that's not all. She picks a theme or a trend, and dresses within that theme for the week! She'll pick a theme like "leopard" or "flannel," and throughout the week, each one of those outfits will fit within that theme. People look to her for teacher styles and can shop her looks! She utilizes platforms that allow her to link outfits and accessories, and she makes extra cash through affiliate link purchases! A message from April:

Figure 8.11 April Graves, Teacher Style Influencer.
Source: https://www.shopltk. com/explore/Aprilalldae, last accessed under July 25, 2022

"For years, coworkers would (and still do) ask why was I so dressed up and where was I going. My reply, "To my classroom!" Then they'd

inquire about the places where I like to shop. So I finally realized, there might be a l'il hustle in all of this! Since I'm getting dressed for work anyway, why not make it work for me! That was my thought when I finally decided to take two things that I love (fashion and teaching) and put them on full display in a way that could possibly drop a few extra coins in my (fashionable) pocket. Needless to say, it's super-fun and fulfilling."

https://www.shopltk.com/explore/Aprilalldae

PASSION ALERT: TEACHER BLING

Amber Drummond, Owner of Teacher Blingz N Tingz

Amber Drummond (@teacher_blingzntingz) is a teacher who has a flare for bling! She took her love for all things sparkly and created a business that offers the most precious charms that can be added to teacher lanyards and badges (Figures 8.12–8.14). The charms come in just about any object you can imagine, and she even has an option to customize them. A message from Amber:

"Being able to express my bright personality and my love for education into one has always been a goal of mine. I'm not your typical teacher, so I thought, "Why not have my badge holder stand out just like my personality?" Giving teachers the option to personalize their badge holder with bling and charms that represent what they love most is very rewarding to me. I, like many of my other teacher friends, absolutely love being a teacher, but we are so much more. I've been able to create badges that speak to the many roles we play. The badge holders we create do everything from helping teachers remember a lost loved one to someone who wanted their badge to match the decor of their classroom. That in itself is super-rewarding!"

https://www.teacherblingzntingz.com/

Figure 8.12 Amber's lanyard charms.
Source: https://www
.teacherblingzntingz.com/, last
accessed under July 25, 2022

Figure 8.13 Amber Drummond, Owner of Teacher
Blingz N Tingz.
Source: https://www
.teacherblingzntingz.com/, last
accessed under July 25, 2022

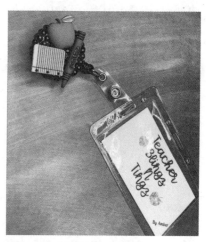

Figure 8.14 Amber's
lanyard charms.
Source: https://www
.teacherblingzntingz.com/, last
accessed under July 25, 2022

PASSION ALERT: STORYTELLING AND RELATIONSHIPS

Matt Halpern, Founder Matt Halpern Education

Matt Halpern (@matthalperneducation) is a teacher who "flowed into teaching." According to his website, after starting his career in the business field, the events of September 11, 2001, had him reevaluating his entire life. He quit his corporate job and went back to school for teaching! Twenty-some years later and he defines himself as an early childhood aficionado! He says that building relationships is the foundation of his work, both with children and adults (Figures 8.15–8.17). He is a fierce advocate for social justice and equity in all classrooms. He said that after a few years of teaching second grade, he was moved to kindergarten, where he found himself overflowing with anecdotes and stories. As he began sharing them with others, one thing flowed to another and he's written his first professional book, *A Teacher's Guide to Interactive Writing*, with Heineman Publishing! He has transformed his love for storytelling and building relationships into books, speaking engagements, and even his own merchandise. A message from Matt:

> *"Presenting, consulting, and writing as a side hustle became a little too much to juggle with being a full-time classroom teacher, so I finally made the leap to working for myself full-time. However, I knew I wanted to stay involved with instruction. So, in addition to presenting and working in schools with teachers, I also teach and tutor virtually a few hours a week which lets me stay active with teaching practices and try new ideas out with students. Working for myself has been a massive shift, but I genuinely feel like I'm impacting teachers and students, just in a different way. My passion in the classroom was social-emotional learning and writing, and those are the areas where I've focused my business. Find your area of expertise and run with it."*

https://www.matthalperneducation.com/

Figure 8.15 Matt's book.
Source: https://www
.matthalperneducation
.com/, last accessed under
July 25, 2022

Figure 8.16 Matt Halpern,
Founder Matt Halpern
Education.
Source: https://www
.matthalperneducation.com/, last
accessed under July 25, 2022

Figure 8.17 Matt's merch.

PASSION ALERT: EMPOWERING AND INSPIRING EDUCATORS

Tiffaney Whyte, Owner De'AvionBlu

De'AvionBlu Innovations is owned and operated by Tiffaney Whyte (Figures 8.18 and 8.19). According to her website, Tiffaney is a special education teacher and single mother who finally decided to go for her dreams of designing shirts for her fellow educators who are just as excited and passionate about this profession as she is! Her designs are all about making sure educators feel uplifted and empowered. Teachers are sure to find motivation and inspiration from one of her original T-shirt designs. A message from Tiffaney:

"In 2018, I was having a tremendously hard year teaching. I felt discouraged and overlooked. I was being questioned about my teaching style and ethics. I needed something to encourage me and bring back my zest for teaching. So, I created this brand to help myself and my fellow educators feel proud, empowered, and motivated about cultivating young minds. De'AvionBlu was created out of me feeling defeated and needing something to help me gain back feeling empowered. Not only am I a proud and passionate advocate for the education field, but I also believe in the importance of being a successful Black business owner. Do what makes you happy, create joy for yourself! When you find that keep going and don't stop! One thing that brings me great joy in this teaching profession is every Monday for the entire school year I include yellow in my wardrobe because teaching can be stressful! I started a movement on social media and encouraged other educators to join in on wearing yellow. Knowing that I have been able to encourage other educators brings me the joy that I needed!" Join us by using the hashtag #TeachersWearYellowOnMonday and spread some JOY!

https://deavionbluinnovations.com/

Figure 8.18 Tiffaney Whyte, Owner De'AvionBlu.
Source: https://deavionbluinnovations.com/, last accessed under July 25,2021

Figure 8.19 Tiffaney's t-shirt design.

TIPS FOR GETTING STARTED

- Think about something you're really passionate about, even if it's not teaching-related.
- Find a platform like Etsy, Shopify, or your own website to start selling on.
- Collaborate with friends and others to help you promote your idea.
- Talk about your product so people know it exists! Don't be afraid to talk about your passion openly and often.

Chapter 9
Exit Ticket

3-2-1 Exit Ticket	
3	Things I Want to Remember
2	Things that Might Be a Challenge
1	Question I Still Have

Okay, friends. We hope that as this book is coming to a close for you, you are brimming with many ideas . . . or at least just one. We have highlighted many ways that an educator like you can turn your educational expertise into extra income. Our intent was to share our journeys in order to help you to see that if it's what you're seeking, you are skilled enough to do things outside of the classroom that bring you both joy and extra money.

Don't feel disappointed if you only have one idea right now. That's where we started. Keep this book close by to help you add on more profitable ideas if and when you're ready. We both started creating resources before we ever had blogs, websites, or social media platforms to promote them on. We simply started to create. We put work out there that we thought would be helpful to other educators.

One thing that we want you to understand is that one thing can lead to another. Starting one project can make the next project come together seamlessly. Looking back on our journey, we see that our merch, courses, and memberships were easier to put into place after we'd established our online presences and built up a library of resources over the years. Speaking engagements were born because we created a resource, told a story, and shared it on the internet. It's honestly like tipping dominoes. You'll find the progression that works for you. You just have to get started.

Please don't think we are hitting you with all of this information and then releasing you on your own, into the wild, while we ride off into the distance. So, let's meet up for a coffee date one final time before we send you on your way. In the following sections we separately offer our advice for some different states you might be in as an educator seeing this book coming to an end and feeling . . .

UNSURE WHERE TO START?

LaNesha's Advice

Start with nailing your niche. At the end of the day, you want to have a purpose to return to when you feel like giving up or if it gets hard. For example, my "why" is summed up in the following statement:

> *I help primary educators make ALL subjects globally relevant, authentic, and FUN so that students grow to be independent workers and critical thinkers. Educators will get ideas, resources, and a community of like-minded teachers who truly believe that their students will change the world.*

That's my *why*. That's the statement I return to when I am feeling lost or overwhelmed. That statement encompasses all of the work that I do with social studies, writing, and reading because of the *way* that I've set those resources up. That even informed the sayings that I've created for T-shirts! If I'm presented with an opportunity, I will go back to my mission statement and ask myself if it aligns. It doesn't matter if you haven't created a single thing; create your mission that you will manifest one day. Once you have that, you're going to become hyper-focused on making things that align with your niche.

Creating this will keep you from starting a bedazzled teacher pencil bag line one day and science flashcards the next. I'm not saying you can't do all these things, but if you are trying to be the "go-to" voice for a topic or way of teaching (or way of living), then the more streamlined you can become, the better, especially when you're first starting out. If you are a science teacher who makes amazing flashcards, be that for a while. Grow your audience. Create great content. Then, if you decide that your passion for bedazzled pencil bags is still something you want to do, then you'll already have a group of supporters ready to receive it. You'll probably even come up with some cool science-related designs for your sparkly pencil bags!

Someone will want what you've got. There have been so many times in my life when I needed something that I didn't know how to or feel like creating. I've been so grateful to people all over the world who've created the perfect tee for my children's birthday celebrations or a customizable printable family planner. Using your creativity and your gifts is allowed for educators. It happens all over the world in tons of other industries, and we can do it, too. How many chefs work at a restaurant but cater special events on their own? There are hairstylists who do hair but have also created courses on how to achieve and master a specific haircut and color strategy. The moral of the story is, you can use your talents, gifts, and knowledge to create resources in creative ways if you give it a try.

Naomi's Advice

My advice to you would be to start in the place that brings you the most joy! For me, I have to be excited about the work I'm doing in order to be motivated to finish it. I want to add that whatever you start with would probably be best paired with social media. If you want to make merch, social media will help you get eyes on it. If you want to create a course, social media can help you find people interested in signing up. If you want to create resources, social media can help you talk about what you've created.

As you were reading this book, was there one idea that was really calling your name? Was there one idea that you have the tools to make happen right now? Go with that one.

TOO MUCH WORK FOR TOO LITTLE MONEY?

We decided to speak to this section for two reasons:

1. We wanted to be transparent (while also not telling *all* of our business), and

2. We are vastly different in what motivates us to make extra money.

We figured that if we were this different, most of the people who read this book will fall closer to one of our sides on the spectrum. We have friends who have disclosed the amounts they make from monetizing their educational expertise that are all across the board. We have friends who are beyond thrilled and bring in an extra $90 dollars every week and friends who have made over $35OK in one year on a well-established membership. We have a friend who makes about $500 dollars a month on resources. And another who made $20,000 in one weekend after launching a successful course. The income that is possible is all over the place. What you can walk away with is the notion that if you are here to use your passions, gifts, and knowledge to make money, then the sky is the limit.

LaNesha's Advice

For me, when things seem too out of reach or impossible, I shut down. When I hear that someone is making hundreds of thousands of dollars on something that I'm also doing, my mind goes to "Well, that's so far away from what I'm making, so what's the point." I'm not saying this is good, I'm saying this is the way my mind works. I have to make a conscious effort to push past this. When I first started, I was inspired by the stories of people who were having fun while bringing in enough money to pay off some debt. My husband and I really wanted to pay down a student loan, and so it was really fun to be able to take the extra $100 or $200 a month and chuck it at the debt. Here's the thing: the more you create and the more you expand, the more opportunities you have to make the amount of money that you want. For the longest time, my goal was $700 a month. That would allow us to have an extra hundred on our "fun" budget and I was able to pay for my daughter's ballet lessons (and slippers, and tutus, and recital outfits . . . dance moms get it). Once I hit and started to surpass that goal, I had to begin to take my business seriously. The thing about this work is that it isn't always consistent. We have seasons that make us squeal with excitement. There have been plenty of four-figure months and even a few five-figure months. There are other times where we are barely able to cross over four figures. The consistency is the thing that makes this tricky. If you are okay with this idea, then I am of the belief that "any extra money is good money!"

Naomi's Advice

Unlike my bestie LaNesha, hearing the amounts that are possible to make is a huge motivator for me. I haven't ever made $350,000 in one year, but knowing that it's a possibility has me thinking, "say less." That's all I need to know to stay motivated. I'm not foolish enough to think that income like that is just going to fall into my lap out of nowhere, but numbers like that motivate me and help me remember that there's always room to grow and improve.

This was a big draw for me, if you remember my journey of how I got started. I wanted to create resources like a coworker had suggested, but when I thought about the time it would take versus the take-home, I didn't think it was worth it. I was still in the classroom at the time, and my time outside of work was precious.

Now, this isn't to say that I am only in it for the money. If you knew me well enough, you'd know this couldn't be further from the truth. My resources are fairly priced and well put together. But if I am going to be investing the 40+ hours a week that I do into all the branches of my business, I want to know that it's going to be worth it and that my hard work, creativity, and time spent will be rewarded. I am in it for *some* money. This is my job. I need to earn money to help support my family and live my life. So hearing the numbers that other people are capable of earning in a week, or a month, or a year have always been #goals for me. I am of the belief, "If they can do it, I can do it, too."

WANT TO JUMP INTO 10 IDEAS AT ONCE AND JUST CAN'T DECIDE?

LaNesha's Advice

"Now you know that's a recipe for disaster. Pick one thing and sit down." Naomi wrote that as a comedic placeholder for me to write this chapter, but I'm leaving it because #facts. This is where Naomi and I differ. As you'll see in the following, she's the queen of juggling 30 things at once. That makes me want to close my laptop, open Netflix, and press Play on the next episode of my favorite show (*Peaky Blinders*). I just can't! My brain doesn't work that way. I'm envious of Naomi because she knows how to get it done and get it done quickly, but I need more of a plan before moving forward. If you are ready to jump in and do all the things, I would advise you to make a list of all the things and then do some ranking. I would encourage you to place a "1" next to the things that you have a clear vision for and you can't wait to get going. Then, place a "2" next to the items that thrill you, but you haven't figured out the logistics. Then, the "3s" are going to be the things that you'll get to eventually. Then, rewrite the list with the 1s on top, followed by the 2s and 3s. Now you will get to do all the things, but you're going to have a loose roadmap to help you know where to begin and what can come next.

Naomi's Advice

You sound like me! I know the feeling. And I often have several projects going on all at once. I can make it work, but it can honestly be overwhelming and stressful at times. In my mind, all of these things can be connected. If you have a social media presence where you've made yourself the authority on a few things, you can create resources on the same topics. Once you have enough resources, you can add them to a membership. As more people come to enjoy you and what you have to share through your social media, you might realize it's time to start planning a course, creating merch, or pitching yourself to some conferences. And then somewhere in there you may get the itch to write a book about one of the many wonderful things you have going on or just something that is close to you personally.

Lucky for me, I have a partner like LaNesha who can keep me on course when I start to get all over the place. Even though I can thrive on juggling multiple ideas at once, a lot of the time, I would be better off focusing on one at a time. Or prioritizing them like she suggested.

One more thing to consider is how seasonal some ideas and projects can be. Depending on the time of year that you are deciding to get started, one idea may make more sense than another right now. Your idea for a *Back to School Educator Gift Box* (feel free to take that idea) may have to wait if it's currently the middle of February. Tabling that idea and coming back to it later might make more sense.

DON'T HAVE THE TIME?

We want to acknowledge the fact that we are fully aware that we do not all have the same 24-hours in a day. Some people have childcare and others do not. Some have partners who can help with dinner and cleaning, and some do not. Some have medical issues to attend to (their own or someone they care for), and others do not. Some are juggling multiple jobs and others are not. Some have disabilities and others do not. Some have access to technology that others do not. And some have certain privileges that others do not. We aren't all the same and our time is not the same, often due to circumstances outside of our control.

LaNesha's Advice

Oh, my goodness. This one is tough. Because you're right . . . who has time? In theory, we all "don't have time," but in all honesty, I also don't have time to scroll social media or catch up on my latest reads, either. But I want to. So I do. This, this is precisely why we wanted to mention the concept of passion over and over in this book. Passion is what drives you. I remember being up late one night creating a resource that I was so excited about. My husband was getting in bed while I was sitting up on my laptop. He looked at me and said, "I don't think I've ever been passionate about something enough to make me stay up late and work like that." I laughed and worked for another 30 minutes before turning in. While that's not true anymore for him today (he's all into real estate now), it made me realize the power of passion. No way would I stay up late and work on something that I wasn't super-passionate about. That is what drove me to want to create! I don't know what gets released when you're passionate about something—dopamine, endorphins—but whatever it is, it's a great feeling. This is why you have to find something that you love and figure out how to get creative with it.

As far as working while balancing friends, family, children, and so on, I'm fairly similar to Naomi, so you'll get the gist of that part in the following. On a more logistical level, for me, it is about balance. And, honestly, I'm one to talk because I've had tons of years with no balance, but that is really what helped me. There would be times where I'd set a timer and grind out a project or a blog post on a daily basis, but sometimes I would have to move in seasons. By that, I would tell my family something like, "Hey, I have a big project coming up in two weeks. I really need to be focused for those days, but after that, I'm taking a two-week break." So instead of a daily grind, it was a seasonal grind. For those weeks, my family and friends offered to step up and support with dinners or pick-ups/drop-offs and I'm forever grateful for them. If that is an option for you, lean on your village. Don't be afraid to ask for extra support for a period of time. If that isn't an option for you and you are only able to work in small doses, then remember that this isn't a race. You aren't going to get a trophy for finishing a project quickly. You'll get there; stay the course.

Naomi's Advice

I hear you. I do. I have been juggling my business ventures through different stages of my life. No kids + working full time in the classroom, 2 kids + working full time in the classroom, 2 kids + working full time from home with 1 of those kids. And that's not even counting having to go grocery shopping, planning and cooking dinner, cleaning, having time to myself, spending time with my husband, making time for friends, and stressing about how much water I've drunk for the day. It can be a lot. It can be overwhelming. I know everyone uses their 24 hours in a variety of ways.

I'll share two things that have helped me:

1. Make time for this venture even if 30 minutes a day is all you can devote. I've recently created a time of the day that I've nicknamed "Naomi's Power Hour." It varies based on when and if my son takes a nap. Some days it's a Power 39 Minutes, but I've made my peace with that. I put my phone away, grab a little snack, and work like there's no tomorrow. You would be surprised at how much you can accomplish in short bursts. Don't count yourself out because you don't have a three-hour block to devote to a task. Start something and add to it a little bit each day.

2. Having friends that I can be accountable to and with. Partnering up with other creators can help you get work accomplished by dividing and conquering what needs to get done. You can also ask a friend to check in on your progress to help you stay motivated and on task. Friends and other creators can also double as feedback-givers and product-testers!

AFRAID TO PUT YOURSELF OUT THERE?

LaNesha's Advice

Don't operate from a place of "What will people think?" but rather work from a mental place of "How can my gifts positively affect someone else?" because that is what we are really doing here! Someone is always going to hate what you do. You're going to dream too big for some people. Haters exist. Where is your energy going to go? Are you going to live life trying to appease a faceless group of people called "they"? Are you going to wait for "their" approval? Because let me tell you, that'll likely never come. I read a really great quote on social media that basically said to let people think you're "cringeworthy" if they need to. Everyone's version of "cringe" is personal, so how are you going to show up and not be cringy? Someone will *always* have something to say. And, of course, your supporters will be plentiful, but you know how it feels to get your evaluation back from your boss and everything is highly effective or effective except one thing. You fixate on that one thing. It doesn't matter that everything else was basically perfect; our human nature often makes us dwell on the one negative. Business is no different. You have to move forward and learn to take criticism with a grain of salt. You're putting yourself in a vulnerable position when you put your work out into the world.

You will undoubtedly make mistakes, but that's a part of it. I'd rather make mistakes on something I tried than to have never taken the risk.

Naomi's Advice

When you are walking in your purpose and moving in your passion, what does what anyone else has to say have to do with you? As long as you aren't going against your personal values and no one is being harmed, do what makes you happy. Don't let the fear of what others think or might say keep you from following your dreams. Also, we have gotten our fair share of pushback. It comes with the territory. You learn to brush it off and keep it moving toward your goals.

It sounds cheesy, but even on a beautiful, warm, sunny day, you're going to have some people who love it, some people who wish it were raining, and some who wish it were cold. You can't be everything to everybody, and you'll burn yourself out real quick if you waste time trying.

I'm not for everyone, and that's okay. As a recovering people pleaser, that was hard to type. But I know that it's true and keeping that in the forefront of my mind has served me well.

READY TO START RIGHT NOW?

LaNesha's Advice

Yaaaaassss!!! Let me be the first to say "You GO, THEN!!!" Shoot, tag me on your first resource/product/book or whatever and let me be the first to shout you out. If you stepped out on faith and made a dream of yours come true, then I'm screaming at the top of my lungs for you. The feeling that comes with knowing that you have changed someone's life or education career for the better, well, very little compares to that. You have so much to offer the world. I know you do because otherwise you wouldn't even be in this profession. I would also advise you to take a moment and remember this feeling of excitement and hope. You'll be able to think back on this moment for years to come and celebrate this version of yourself. I'm so happy for you!

Naomi's Advice

I am *so* proud of you! Follow that passion and make that money, honey! Being able to make an impact in and outside of the classroom has been a dream come true for me, and I am sure you'll find the same thing to be true of your experience as well. I'm thankful to be able to work from home with my son and make enough to help support my family while I'm out of the classroom. I love being able to continue to help educators and students in a different capacity. Whether you are in or outside of a school setting right now, you can still have a powerful impact on the education world.

No one can share your ideas the way you can. No one is going to design a course, shirt, or resource the way you would. Your voice is needed. Your knowledge is valuable. I am so excited for you! Go get started.

Index

Note: Page reference f indicates to figure.